Mary W. Paxton

Miss Elvester's Girls

Vol. 2

Mary W. Paxton

Miss Elvester's Girls
Vol. 2

ISBN/EAN: 9783337346393

Printed in Europe, USA, Canada, Australia, Japan

Cover: Foto ©Thomas Meinert / pixelio.de

More available books at **www.hansebooks.com**

BY

THE AUTHOR OF 'BY-WAYS.'

IN THREE VOLUMES.

VOL. II.

LONDON: TINSLEY BROTHERS,

8 CATHERINE STREET, STRAND, W.C

1 8 8 3.

COLSTON AND SON, PRINTERS, EDINBURGH.

CONTENTS.

CHAPTER VIII.

MISS ELVESTER'S GIRLS.

CHAPTER I.

THE BRAE.

'Near some fair town I'd have a private seat,
  Built uniform—not little, nor too great ;
  Better if on a rising ground it stood—
  On this side fields, on that a neighbouring wood.
    . . . .
  A little garden, grateful to the eye,
  And a cool rivulet run murmuring by ;
  On whose delicious banks a stately row
  Of shady limes or sycamores should grow.'

'MAN is born to trouble, as the sparks fly upwards.' If there is not this to come between him and perfect peace, then there will be that.

When Miss Elvester got to know exactly
how she stood, she was relieved to find that
she should be able to make ends meet—and
even tie—with much less straining of them
than she had at first supposed would be
necessary. No sooner, however, were her
housekeeping anxieties so far allayed, than
care of a different kind sprang up to dis-
turb her.

A change had passed over Ursula. No
more repinings were heard, nor high words
about family and claims of birth—nothing was
thought of but stern duty now-a-days. And
duty, as Ursula conceived of it, was the doing
of whatever one most particularly disliked to
do; for according to this, her new theory of
the universe, a schooling of herself to suffering was the chief thing here required of man.
So it had come about that the very young
person who, a few months ago, would have
maintained that no lady ought ever to undertake any kind of work which could sully the
delicate whiteness of her fingers, was ready
now, should nobody interfere, to roughen

her pretty hands beyond all recognition by assisting Mysie in the coarsest household drudgery.

But, as it happened, there was somebody to interfere : though Ursula had taken this surprising leap from one extreme to its opposite, Miss Elvester kept the balance midway, as she had always done ; so she told her girl that, while it was proper to engage to a certain extent in practical domestic economy, the idea carried to the proposed length would be a piece of the most fantastic absurdity, and, in short, need never be mentioned at The Brae.

Ursula, of course, felt that she was very cruelly misunderstood ; but just in time she remembered that here, too, in submission to a well-intentioned if mistaken elder sister's notions of propriety, lay the path of duty—the opportunity for self-negation. But occupation of some salutary nature she must have ; so she busied herself with plain sewing, which she did not love—studied ' Bishop Butler's Sermons,' which she could not comprehend ; also ' Ranke's History of the Popes,' which she took no human interest in ; attended a weekly drawing-room prayer-meeting at Baronshaugh, which the more she tried to profit by, so much the more she loathed. And all this in addition to her primary business, the instructing of Ulrica. If she had been a Romanist she would have entered a convent; if an Anglican, she would have joined a sisterhood. But Presbyterianism will have no such cutting of the difficult knot by troubled souls within her fold. She will have them remain in their providentially-appointed places, quietly doing their work there, and waiting, watching, praying, till the light comes.

In the end of January Christian paid a visit to her sisters ; and Christian was pleased with the new house quite up to the expectation of Ulrica, who acted as show-woman. The dining-room was so cosy ; the drawing-room, containing whatever things of beauty had been saved from the wreck, was exactly what the drawing-room of such a toy house ought to be. As for the little bedchambers upstairs, how could Jenny, with the scanty means at her command, have succeeded in making such daintily pretty places of them ? Then the garden— it was not a conventional garden in the least, but possessed an individuality of its own, quaint and refreshing. Just now, to be sure, it was little more than a framework for future foliage ; but in due season what verdant bushiness there would be—what bursting into blossom—what a glow of fruit and bloom !

Entering through a screen of lilacs, you went up and on (for the ascent did not stop with the house), till both brae and garden terminated in a plantation of birches, poplars, and laburnums. The rustic bower placed here was a famous observatory. Perched so high, you saw Laighbield far down in the hollow to the left, with the river winding between it and you ; on the other hand, you had a fir-topped hill, a brambly thicket, and a runaway burn ; while before you spread out fields and fields, specked with white farm-steads here and there; and yonder in the distance, rimming the horizon with silver, glimmered the sea-line of the Auchterbrechan coast.

' So this is the state called poverty ? ' said Christian on the evening of her home-coming, placing herself, as of old, close to Miss Elvester's side, that she might stroke the hair or pinch the ear of that lady, or take any other sisterly liberty that might occur to her. ' If I had not been told I should not have guessed it.'

' Poverty has several circles,' it was answered; ' ours is the outer one, where the flowers still blow, though with a subdued colour and diminished fragrance.'

' But oh, what a change from Eastravoe ! ' said Ursula sadly. ' We Shetlanders have the *mal du pays* as badly as the Swiss; and one sometimes grows sick with longing for—' She suddenly checked herself, and instead of finishing as she had intended, added,—' But we have no right to complain.'

Nobody but herself was showing any disposition to complain. It is noticeable, though, that whenever people prone to grumble feel the folly of it, they kindly include the rest of the company in their own condemnation, saying, — '*We* should study contentment;' '*we* ought not to repine;' 'it would become *us* to be thankful for so many mercies.'

'The Brae is quite different in every way from Eastravoe,' said Ulrica. 'Ursula and I make ourselves very useful now. Mysie is a good, strong servant; but one person can't do everything in an establishment like ours. She thinks she could, but we won't let her, because we are quite certain she would undermine her constitution.'

'Christian will please observe that "we" are as wise as ever, and as fond of sounding words,' said Miss Elvester.

'You will be happy to know that my friend, Mrs Smillie, has been a good deal impressed by you,' Christian informed Ulrica. 'She calls you "The little girlie that speaks like the dictionary."'

'Ursula and I don't take much account
of Mrs Smillie,' replied Ulrica; 'she is quite
an ignorant person.'

'So are we ourselves,—hopelessly ignorant,' said Ursula.

And Christian looked at her to see if she
were in jest; but no; the beautiful, proud
face was only too serious to-night.

'Mrs Smillie is *not* ladylike,' insisted
Ulrica.

'Mrs Smillie is good, and that is better
than being ladylike,' said Christian.

'One might be both,' observed Ulrica.

'One might, of course. Mrs Smillie
hasn't forgotten Slyboots, Ulrica. Only
last week she made the kindest inquiries
about him.'

'Did she, indeed? Well, Slyboots is in
robust health physically; but morally he is a
waste; for, oh, Christian, though I have taken
every care with him, and have tried and tried
to bring him up well, he is really a depraved
cat at the core. There was a darling little
robin which used to come to our back windows

for crumbs. It got so tame that it would hop on to my hand and look up at me with its cunning little head to one side, so saucily. But you will never see that bird, Christian. One morning wicked Slyboots killed and ate him. I hated Slyboots for many hours after, till I began to think it might have been jealousy that drove him to do such a dreadful thing. He might have been afraid of my liking the robin more than I liked him.'

' But if he were only jealous, he needn't have eaten your robin,' suggested Christian.

' No, indeed, he needn't ; I did not think of that. He is low-minded in another way, too,' she went on pathetically. ' He steals everything he can. Jenny says it is an hereditary vice ; so, perhaps, that is some excuse. I try not to love him, because it can't be right to love a thief when you know he is a thief, and won't repent. But then he is such a beauty ; and I am sure, besides, he is a cat with a fine intellect. Jenny says we have no business to overlook crime because of beauty and intellect ; but I can't help forgiving Slyboots.   Have you any pets, Christian ? '

' Willie Ruthven is a great pet,' said Christian.

' I wonder how you can live in hateful Netherlaw !' cried Ulrica, rather apart from the point, as it seemed.

' Netherlaw is not so hateful,—not when you get used to it.'

' Not so hateful !   Netherlaw !   Do you hear her, Jenny ? '

' To tell the truth, it's chiefly you that I hear,' replied Miss Elvester.

' Chapel Street and Argyll Gardens are very different places,' explained Christian.

' Ours is such a pleasant house, too ; and I don't believe any one of you could live with Mrs Cassillis and still hate Netherlaw.'

It did not please Ulrica that ' our ' should be used in such a connection ; so she rather spitefully rejoined,—

' How can you be so fond of everybody ? People who like everybody can't like *any* body very, very much.   And, I daresay, he isn't at all a nice little child that Willie, if only one knew him all round.'

'Oh, but he is though; very much better worth loving than your artful Slyboots.'

'We will rather converse about the people who interest you so much than about Slyboots. I suppose you are fond of Mrs Cassillis of Baronshaugh too?'

'Not very.'

'I'm glad to hear it; neither am I, neither is Jenny; and oh, I was *so* disappointed in the lad.'

'In Quentin Cassillis? What business is he of yours?'

'Look at my head, and you may easily know what business he is of mine. I have a large organ of benevolence, so that I can't help interesting myself in people. I had such hopes about Mr Cassillis (Mr Cassillis and *you*) till I saw him; then I gave them up. Every time we meet he says the very same thing,—"Do you think you are going to like Laighbield? I hope you are, you know." And now he has got to add,—

"And is the Baronshaugh Gallery comfortable? I must come some Sabbath day
and see you in it, you know." But
he won't come,—his mamma won't let
him.'

Christian wanted to know how her sisters
had got into the Baronshaugh Gallery at
all.

'I pay a rent, which the laird's mother
hands over to her church's sustentation fund,'
said Miss Elvester. 'There is a spoiling-of-
the-Egyptians sort of ring about the trans-
action which gives joy to her.'

'People here hate the laird's mother,'
began Ulrica ; 'they say—'

'Don't, dear,' interposed Ursula. 'People
here say very dreadful things ; but we need
not put ourselves on a level with them, by
repeating their idle stories.'

'It must be owned,' said Miss Elvester,
'that the Laighbieldites have not, as a rule,
any notion of proper respect for the powers
that be. They are the sons and grandsons
of men who, in the days of Chartism, had

to fly the country for sedition ; and even at the present time, search all Scotland over, and you will not find a more radical little rookery than this same Laighbield.'

' Oh, they are impertinent!' exclaimed Ulrica. ' Think of this, Christian (it isn't an idle story, Ursula, but something I heard with my own very ears), Jenny and I went one day to be shown through Langbiggin's bonnet factory, and when Jenny asked at the gate for Mr Langbiggin, the old foreman went to the office door and called out, " Hey, Davy! here's folk wanting you." '

Christian smiled.

' I have heard a variety of stories of that kind about Laighbield,' she said.

' And who has told them to you ? '

' Why ?—have you the copyright ? '

' No ; but now I shall find out who talks to you, and what they talk about. Does Captain Cassillis tell you those stories, Christian ? '

' Some of them, I daresay.'

'Describe Captain Cassillis ; you've never mentioned him yet.   Is he a beautiful man ?'

' No, indeed ; not at all beautiful.'

' Has he a handsome figure, then ? '

' Well, yes ; I suppose he has.'

' Tell us—won't you ?—tell us all about him.'

' I can't, knowing so little myself.'

' And yet you've been living in the same house all these weeks ? '

' I suppose I'm not like you, dear.   I haven't a large organ of benevolence. Besides, I had nothing to do with Captain Cassillis, and I had my own affairs to attend to.'

' Christian is not a guest at Argyll Gardens, but a governess,' said Ursula.

Ulrica also was aware of this, but she felt convinced that governess as well as guest must have an opinion about all the inmates of a house.   And what sense was there in holding the opinion back ?

' Do you like Captain Cassillis as much as you like your Willie ? ' she asked.

Christian unaccountably reddened ; Ursula looked shocked ; both exclaimed in a breath,—

'*Ulrica !*'

And Miss Elvester said,—

'That organ which you miscall benevolence leads you astray sometimes. You don't seem to know where exactly laudable interest ends and impertinent curiosity begins. But let me take the liberty of assuring you, my dear, that our curiosity is far more annoying to others than our interest is flattering.'

Snubbed on all hands, Ulrica subsided into silence, and sat ruminating through the rest of the evening upon the puzzle. What could there be about Captain Cassillis which made Christian object even to mention his name ?

CHAPTER II.

SIBYLLINE.

'Then sit ye doon, my bonnie doo,
And in this palm o' mine,
Crossed wi' a siller piece, ye'll lay
That gentle hand o' thine.'

MANY of the Laighbield houses had been built in the time of the window-tax, when economical proprietors saved money by stinting themselves of sunlight. The Brae, however, was none of these; it, fortunately, was blessed with plenty of windows. The drawing-room had three—one looking down the lane by which the house was approached, the other two across the little clover park, which bounded The Brae on its Laighbield

side to the lime-tree road, the river, the
meadow, and the meal-mill.

Just now the river was frozen, and the
landscape encrusted with snow—the finest
snow, like the sugar-coating of a bridecake
—which sparkled but did not melt under
the rays of a sun that might be gazed at by
other than eagle's eyes unblinkingly.

On the day following her arrival, Christian
stood looking out upon this winter scene.
She saw a visitor draw near. The lady
walked remarkably well, and carried herself
with a wonderful degree of dignity for a
person of her inches. There could be but
one such in a parish, and Christian turned
to the only other occupant of the room to
ask,—

'Whom have we here, Jenny? Isn't it
Mrs Brackenburn?'

Miss Elvester raised her head from her
lace-mending, threw a glance outside, and
answered that it was.

' I can now understand the feelings of
Mrs Cassillis of Baronshaugh,' said Chris-

tian. 'Her idea is that ministers' wives
ought to wear things that don't fit, and
bonnets four years out of fashion; but this
one has velvets and sables, and a saucy
little plumed hat, and the look of a person
who only patronises the most fashionable
artists in dress.'

While speaking she heard the door of the
adjoining room—where Ulrica's studies were
in progress—being opened, and then saw
Ursula go down to the gate and meet Mrs
Brackenburn under the rowan-trees.

'They are fast friends,' said Miss Elvester,
in reply to the look which so unusual a pro-
ceeding on her sister's part evoked from
Christian. 'Day and night are hardly less
alike than these two are. Their mutual
attraction is only to be accounted for by the
rule of contrasts.'

And, entering together, a contrast they
certainly were—she whose beauty everybody
admitted at first glance, and whose exceeding
fairness was made all the fairer by the deep
blackness of her eyebrows, lashes, and hair;

and she whom almost everybody directly set down as plain, and as to whose complexion enemies constantly asserted that it and her hair were exactly of a shade. But even about the appearance of Mrs Brackenburn there could be difference of opinion it seemed, for Christian thought that such a pair of eyes would go far to redeem a less attractive face, and that surely many a prettier woman would willingly (if exchanges of the kind were possible) part with some of her charms if in return she could obtain so abundant and so beautifully-tinted tresses.

Mrs Brackenburn had come, she said, to take possession of Ursula for the day. There was some visiting to be done in the parish; Ursula's company would be hailed 'with great acceptance;' would Ursula come?

'Why, I thought you had resolved to visit the poor of the parish no more for ever,' remarked Miss Elvester.

Mrs Brackenburn laughed, then sighed, then laughed again.

'So I did,' she said. 'But what's the use

of resolving to give anything up if, at the same time, your husband is resolving that you shall carry it on ? Dr Brackenburn compels me to continue my visiting, Miss Elvester.'

' Persuades, I should think, you mean.'

' Persuades or compels, it is the same in effect to me. If he were to bluster, and say, " You must and shall do this thing ?" I would just reply, " I won't," and so end. But he doesn't do that. Oh no ; he puts it in this way, " Do you think it can be right to live for yourself alone ; doing only what you like —what is easy and pleasant to you ? This is an exceptionally severe winter, and in consequence there is more than the usual suffering among our poor. Have these people no claims upon you ? You send food and clothing—that is well ; but personal effort is wanted too. Will you not go to these sufferers—feel with them, try to understand them ? Surely I shall not plead with you in vain ? " That is how my husband lectures me. It is really affecting, you know ;

and I feel how right he is and how wrong I am, and how good I am going to be. This morning I had a homily—I've given you an outline of it—and it moved me so that I was obliged to take instant action ; therefore you see me here. Will you come, Ursula ? Don't you think that what is so proper for me must also be proper for you ? '

' You are the minister's wife, I am nobody ; besides, I ought to be busy at home,' said Ursula.

' Ah, my princess, you don't think you are nobody—not you! And busy at home ; with books do you mean ? '

' I believe I have need to be busy with books.'

' You won't take warning ; you *will* be as blue as Mrs Inverarity of " The Ten Lost Tribes " celebrity.'

' Oh no; but if I had a tenth part of Mrs Inverarity's knowledge how happy I should be.'

' And how sorry I ! One Mrs Inverarity is enough for my powers of endurance. Yon

is a human creature without the shadowiest
notion of what fun is. If you talk nonsense,
you must always be sure to tell her, "*This
is a joke*," upon which she will look over
her spectacles at you, in a curious, pitying
way, and you know she is reflecting that
" The laughter of fools is like the crackling
of thorns beneath the pot."'

'I don't think that I either understand a
joke very well.'

'Candidly speaking, I don't think you do.
But, Ursula, if you must be a Mrs Inverarity,
in mercy spare us some of the details—don't,
don't have your hair strained away from
your face, and knotted up so tightly, that
one's head will ache when one looks at it.'

Ursula assured Mrs Brackenburn that
there was no fear ; and then she went to finish
with Ulrica, for the morning's work must be
finished before she could feel free to accompany her friend.

While she had to wait, Mrs Brackenburn
improved her acquaintance with Christian.
The mirthful breeziness of her manner might

not be becoming a clergyman's wife—very likely it was not—yet it was so genuinely natural that one could hardly wish it changed ; at least if that one were, as in the present instance, a person whose liking Mrs Brackenburn thought it worth while to win.

I am afraid such was the tenor of her discourse to Christian 'that we of Laighbield may be apt to blind you by our brilliancy. Let me prepare you a little. We are not a desperately literary people ; we don't burden our memory with who wrote what, but have a sort of general impression that " John Halifax, Gentleman," is by the author of " Lady Audley's Secret," and " Guy Livingstone " by Thackeray ; and if a few of us should sometime hear of " The Earthly Paradise," we shall be divided in opinion between Dante and Milton. And we are mildly musical : we play drawing-room *morceaux*, and sing what *Punch* calls " Love-Songs for Lunatics," and are happy. But oh, as talkers ! it is there that we excel. Words can't describe how entertaining we

are, or give any adequate idea of our chron-
ologies, genealogies, repetitions, and extra-
neous details. We hunt a subject up and
down, and round and round and about—
such absorbingly interesting subjects, of
course. Where the laird went yesterday,
and with whom; what private matter may
be detaining Mrs Cassillis so long in Netherlaw; how many new bonnets Mrs Brackenburn (the odious little woman!) gets in a
season. And we are, every soul of us, fairly
and fully convinced that the cackle of our small
bourg is the echo of the world. Does the
picture please you, Miss Christian Elvester?'

'But isn't there another side to it, Mrs
Brackenburn?'

'There is. On it, you have Mrs Cassillis,
inquisitor-general; Mrs Inverarity, learned
author; Mr Mungo Mauchline, local poet.'

Christian had heard of Mr Mungo Mauchline, and, remembering Dugald Urquhart and
the 'Trysting Tree,' she inquired,—

'What do you say when the poet asks you
to criticise his verses?'

' I tell him that if I were queen, he should
be laureate,' replied Mrs Brackenburn, laughing. ' Mr Mungo Mauchline has a bee in his
bonnet, as we say here. An odd character to
have in charge of our post - office, do you
think ? But Miss Elvester will tell you that,
outside of his one particular craze, the poet
does his work as well as many a saner man.
Now, I have showed you the reverse side;
do you like it better than the other ? '

' But you have left one figure out,' Miss
Elvester reminded her—' that of Mrs Brackenburn, composer of music.'

Mrs Brackenburn coloured violently.

' Have you heard of that ? ' she exclaimed.
' Truly, men's evil manners live in brass.'

' What! you repent, do you ? '

' I hardly know. My husband was excessively annoyed ; and it may be, my penitence
is more for having made that good man blush
for me, than for having tried to extract some
grains of amusement out of the unspeakable
dreariness of a Braidmoss dinner-party.'

' How exactly *did* you distinguish yourself ?

Rumour credits you with a brilliant improvisation. I heard him, in the shape of the letter-carrier, telling my servant about it the other day ; " and *our* minister's wife," he said proudly, " has a voice would lure the laverock frae the lift." '

' I am obliged to him ; but he made a sad mistake : brilliancy there was none.'

' What was there if not brilliancy ?—but may one ask the question without offence ? '

' Quite without offence, Miss Elvester. I think I am ashamed of myself—I really think so ; and I will do penance by telling you just how wicked I was. (Let me be a beacon to you, Miss Christian Elvester !) Well, then, we were at a dinner-party near Braidmoss. In the long and tedious evening, while the too, too well-known love-songs for lunatics were running their usual course, it was suddenly borne in on me that I would out-Herod Herod, and treat the ladies and gentlemen to something more inane than they had ever listened to yet. My turn having come, I announced, " Wood - warblings : an

entirely new song, by an entirely new composer ; " and, amid solemn silence, chanted
four or five nonsense-jingles, like this :—

" Hark ! in the thicket the blackbird sings,
　Tira-la, tira-la, love me !
The thrush from the thorn her melody flings,—
Oh, the bonnie blue skies above me ! "

I found words as I went along, and the
tune took care of itself. I have no doubt
everybody thought it very satisfactory and
pretty—everybody but my husband and one
other, who saw through the merry fooling.
My husband took no notice then. Later
on he called me to account, and—but I drop
a curtain over *that*. The other acute one
privately informed the hostess that Mrs
Brackenburn had been making game of the
company, and a painful explanation ensued.
I felt myself a pariah for the rest of the
evening. The Rev. Daniel Carnegy, a very
dear friend of mine, looked at me speakingly
every little while, and then at his bride, as if
to say to her, " You can see now—I told you
so ! " and when I chanced to sit down near

her, that sweet woman shuddered.   Mr Carnegy, anxious to preserve his treasure from
contact with pitch, instantly placed himself
between her and me ; then, as he must say
something, he complimented me upon my
voice.   "You have had a precious talent
committed to your trust," he remarked.
" Do you never think of putting your gift
to usury, so to say—turning it to account in
the sacred service of song ?   Have you heard
the sweet female choir which that wonderful
trophy, the converted acrobat, has formed in
Netherlaw?"   I believe it is good, I said ;
but such work is not for me,—though I do
attempt sacred song of the kind that suits
me.   Just now I should very much like to
sing,—

> " *Woe's me that I in Mesech am,*
> *A sojourner so long,*
> *That I in tabernacles dwell,*
> *To Kedar that belong.*
> *My soul with him that hateth peace,*
> *Hath long a dweller been ;*
> *I am for peace, but when I speak,*
> *For battle they are keen.*"

That made my disgrace complete. I should not have said it, and I knew I should not; but sometimes when the fiend says "Speak!" I can *not* keep silence. Mrs Carnegy— but no; I'm not going to make any remarks about Mrs Carnegy, except that she is stone-blindly in love with her husband.'

'Is not that only as it should be?' said Miss Elvester.

'Do you think so? I imagine it is best to have your eyes wide open to a man's faults when you marry him. It must be such a shock, don't you see, when the idol supposed to be wholly gold (if blind, one doesn't even guess about the brass and the iron) is found to have feet of clay. Can't you imagine the situation, Miss Elvester?'

'Not a bit; the thing lies so altogether out of my province,' said Miss Elvester, smiling.

'The first sight of the foot of clay! It is a subject for the painter. If I could paint sufficiently well, I would attempt it. Is it out of your province too?' and Mrs Bracken-burn turned laughingly to Christian.

'Yes,' was the answer; 'for if there are no real gold images to be had, I will go without, I think, rather than have one of clay.'

'Ah! but we do many things, we women, that as girls we little dream of. I used to be quite determined never to marry, if it were not a military hero, who should yearly lay fresh laurels at my feet; yet to-day you see me the wife of a sober country minister, who sends me out, much against my will, to visit the poor of his flock. And I had once a friend whom no ordinary attention from a husband was to satisfy—she was but to wish for a thing, and he to fly to the utmost corner of the earth, Ariel like, to fetch it. That girl married a man who did not care one rush either for her or her wishes. But she would have flown to the world's end for him. Poor thing! she tried hard to win him; only she set about it in the wrong way, sighing, taking no care of her appearance, haunting her husband's footsteps incessantly, like a forlorn ghost; so, of course, it was less than no use. That was how her dream of empire ended.'

'One feels so very sorry for anybody like that,' said Christian thoughtfully. 'But what would have been the right way? How should you have acted in her place?'

'First of all, I would have dressed becomingly, and so have made myself a something pleasant to look at in the house, and then I would have outdone my husband in indifference. I would have been the brightest, merriest woman in the world; and if there had been any other whom he would rather have married when he married me, I would have strained every fibre in me to the very utmost to shine her down. All this might not have succeeded, you know; but the way she went was certain failure.'

The words took a strange hold upon Christian; she could not tell why—not then, but in aftertime they were to recur to her with all the impressive force of a guiding oracle.

'My friend is dead,' continued Mrs Brackenburn, 'and her husband is married again. I hope it may be forgiven me that I

bear malice to the man. I should be sorry
to hear of his doing anything nice, or good,
or grand, because it would take away part of
the pleasure I have in detesting him. Miss
Elvester disapproves of malice, I see. She
thinks I use over-strong language, and likes
better the qualified fashion which our lords
have of abusing each other. " He does the
meanest tricks you ever heard of ; but oh,
he's no worse than his neighbours, when all's
said, or, he deserves hanging ; but after all,
he isn't such a bad fellow in the main." '

Before Miss Elvester could answer this,
Ulrica came hastily in, hardly able to acknow-
ledge the stranger's presence, so eager she
was to say,—

' Do, Jenny, let me have a little money.
A spaewife is telling Mysie's fortune ; she
will tell mine too, if I cross her loof with
silver.'

' Which you assuredly shall not do,' was
the unpropitious rejoinder.

' But, indeed, she tells so true,' pleaded
Ulrica, hoping against hope ; ' she says

Mysie's heart is far at sea ; and so it is, you know. And she says there are four sisters in this house—one of them who only lately came, and will soon go — isn't that true too ? She says, besides, that before six more moons shall have waxed and waned, one of us will be a bride ; and if we will all go to her, she will point out which it is to be.'

' My dear child, I won't let either you or Mysie listen to such folly,' said Miss Elvester, rising. ' No, don't follow ; stay where you are till I return. Excuse me, Mrs Brackenburn, I must run to the rescue of my too credulous handmaiden.' And away she went.

' Jenny is so precipitate !' cried the much aggrieved Ulrica. ' That spaewife said she knew more, and could tell more than any-body thought ; and I quite believe it.'

' *I* don't,' said Mrs Brackenburn. ' And if I ever wanted to consult a prophetess, I would choose one who looked impressive and mysterious, not one wearing a tattered Rob Roy shawl and horrible coal-scuttle bonnet, and talking of crossing her loof. But come, Ulrica' (taking the child's hands and drawing her near), 'I will tell your fortune—a quite true fortune—shall I ?'

'But can you ?' said Ulrica sceptically.

'At least as well as the sibyl whom I saw on her way up a few minutes ago, and in whom you trust. I predict that you shall be an authoress; that you shall have all the success you deserve ; that you shall earn a thousand a-year (more or less).'

While Ulrica was turning about in her mind this somewhat doubtful deliverance, Christian jestingly desired that she also might have her fate read.

'Let me study your face, then,' said Mrs Brackenburn. 'Turn to the window—so. Yes ; that will do. Now, look me straight in the eyes. You must have a golden image, or you will have none, do you tell us, Miss Christian Elvester ? Well ; hear me—and believe or not, as you like. Before six more moons have waxed and waned, we'll say, you shall be a bride, and there will be quite as much clay as gold in the object of your idolatry ; also you shall have cause, it is feared, to sing to yourself, ruefully,—" Oh, I wish I didn't love him, or that he'd love me ! " I have spoken.'

' Could you have given me nothing better than that,' said Christian. ' But it will not come to pass, neither within six moons nor ever, I am sure, *sure* that it will not.'

And it did seem a thing impossible, that she should ever be the bride of a man who had given her his name for any other reason than true love of her.

' Are you indeed sure, *sure* that it will not,' mimicked Mrs Brackenburn, mis-chievously smiling. ' Time will tell. But here comes my princess Ursula ; so, as the dear old-fashioned story books have it, let us not anticipate.'

CHAPTER III.

A ROUND OF UNFASHIONABLE CALLS.

'Let not ambition mock their useful toil,
Their homely joys, and destiny obscure;
Nor grandeur hear with a disdainful smile
The short and simple annals of the poor.'

IT was Laighbield 'meal-hour' when Mrs Brackenburn and Ursula left The Brae. A number of girls were sliding on road and river, and roughing it after a fashion peculiar to themselves. One of a group under the lime-trees had the grace to call to her comrades to make way for the ladies.

' Ha'e ye nae bashfu'ness in ye ava, lassies?' she inquired; to which one of the lassies right merrily rejoined,—

'Bashfu'ness ne'er cam' to oor yett but ance, Tibbie, an' that time we werena in.'

'How can they be so boisterous!' exclaimed Ursula, when at a safe distance from the noisy crew. 'Will not anybody teach them better?'

'Anybody may, who feels equal to it,' said Mrs Brackenburn. 'Have you a mind that way? It would be a boon to the community, if you would undertake the manners of the maidens of Laighbield.'

'*I!*' and Ursula shuddered. 'No, no, indeed; not I! for it is one thing to say that this or the other should be done, quite a different thing to go and do it.'

Across the bridge, in front of a weaver's shop, a knot of men had gathered, in animated discussion. So much waving of arms and such a strife of tongues would have led a stranger to imagine that some fierce quarrel was being waged. Not so, however; this was merely the Laighbield parliament, which assembled daily to criticise Her Majesty's Government, and settle what ought to be the policy, home and foreign, of the Cabinet.

'These are they who bother candidates at election times,' remarked Mrs Brackenburn, as she and Ursula approached. 'Hark! the foremost speaker is blowing a blast against the State Church, and none the less loudly that he has caught sight of me. Oh, I like that—'

'We do not seek to deny,' the orator was saying, 'that good men are to be found in its ministry; good men may be found even in the Papacy itself. But what we do and will maintain, uphold, and assert is, that *as a Kirk*, the Establishment is a dried, withered, sapless, fusionless, degenerate institution, with the form of godliness, but denying the power thereof. But the day is now come when Scotland must be delivered from the religion and the gospel of Erastianism; when it must be said, "Away with your fiddling ministers, drinking elders, and dancing Sabbath-school teachers! Down with the iniquity of having national funds appropriated by a faithless,

sycophant sect! Out of the land of the Cov-
enant with liturgies, and read homilies, and
apeings of the flumgummeries of Rome!—"

' Ursula, Ursula! why do you hurry on?'
said Mrs Brackenburn, laughing. ' Isn't it
always well to hear both sides of a question?
And I wanted to know what would come of
that grand climax, but your impatience has
disappointed me.'

But to linger in such a vicinity longer than
could be avoided, was one of the last things
Ursula would have thought of. This phase
of the working-man was new to her; and his
assertion of himself, and outspoken freedom
in assailing time-honoured institutions, scan-
dalised her even more than the bold levity of
the girls had done. So she and her companion left the parliament to deal out dis-
establishment to the National Church, and
went quickly along the Bridgend and into the
main street of the town.

Here they came upon the wife of the
Free Church minister out doing her market-
ing. And Mrs M'Spur, it soon transpired,

had no great respect for the Laighbield
poor.

'The curlers played a match last week for
meal to distribute—the losing side to pay,'
she said; 'and, would you believe it, several
parties sold their share the same day they
got it, for money to drink! They're a
bad set.'

'We are all bad enough,' said Mrs Brackenburn; 'and who expects but that charity
will sometimes be misused?'

Mrs M'Spur opined that misuse of charity
was the rule, and that a great deal of impo-
sition was carried on, and drinking; and as
for greed!

'Just yesterday,' said she, 'Mr M'Spur
was visiting an old wife who seemed to be
at death's door. There was something on
her mind, he could see that, and he thought
it would be a burdened conscience, for she
has been a sore neglector of ordinances this
many a day. But when he put down his
ear to catch the whisper—she could scarcely
speak, mind you — it was just to ask,

" Have you ony odd bawbees about you the
day ? " '

' Poor humanity !' ejaculated Mrs Brackenburn.

'You'll know old Saunders Grubb, the
" rags, bones, gather-away man " ? ' the other
continued ; ' I doubt he is near his last
journey now, poor body ; but he will take
no thought on his past careless ways—he
was another that never darkened a church
door,—and when Mr M'Spur went in to reason with him, the poor hardened creature
flapped the bedclothes up over his face, and
said he, as bold as a trooper, " I am nane
fear't to dee, sir ! "   It is terrible, terrible !'

' Isn't it !' rejoined Mrs Brackenburn ;
'and the celibacy of the clergy would be
sure, if women only guessed what revela-
tions of the depravity of the human heart
a clergyman's wife has in store.'

But the humour of these things appealed
strongly to this little lady, so that it is to
be feared her tone was hardly so sympathetic as it might have been.

Soon parting from Mrs M'Spur, the pair
stopped at the door of a thatched cottage
opposite the parish school, and knocking,
were bidden by the shrill voice of Mistress
Mirren Gillespie to, 'Come awa' in by,'
which they did accordingly.

Mrs Gillespie dusted a pair of chairs with
her apron (they needed no dusting, it was
merely a ceremony), placed them in front
of the fire, and, without a moment's loss of
time, returned to her twofold occupation of
lining bonnets and rocking with the foot a
green-painted wooden cradle containing twin
babies. Mrs Gillespie, to her other virtues,
added that of being 'a capital manager.'
Her kitchen was speckless; the stone-flags
were beautifully sanded; the hearth was
ornamented with an original design in
pipe-clay. Opposite the window stood the
'dresser,' a goodly sight, with its collection
of plates, jugs, bowls, ranged against the
wall, row above row, so as to make the
most satisfactory possible display. At the
side of this grand achievement towered an

eight-day clock. An instructive clock it was:
above the dial-plate glowed an historical painting, John Knox on a vividly crimson mat,
preaching to Mary of Scotland, whose gown
was white satin, and who pensively rested her
elbow on a table, the cover of which was
very greenly green. Behind the queen's
chair of state hung a gold-fringed, bright
blue curtain; in the background were two
attendants, a yellow fiddle, a quite modern
fireplace, and the Reformer's walking-stick.
But even this was not all. The face of the
clock was further illustrated with four notable
portraits: Luther, Calvin, Wishart, and Mel-
ancthon looked out, stern eyed, each from
his corner. But in spite of this outward
fair show,—

'She's nane to be lippened to, that ane,'
said Mrs Gillespie; 'she'll rin twa hours
fast i' the week, sae wull she.'

The sex of the clock, however, surely
sufficiently accounted for this rushing to
conclusions sooner than reason was.

Mrs Brackenburn was here now to ask

after the progress of her pupil Tommy,
who had broken his arm on a slide a few
days ago.

'Tommy gaed back to his wark yestreen,'
said Mrs Gillespie sententiously.

'From what I heard, I expected to find
him still in bed,' said the visitor.   'Are
you quite sure he was fit to go out?'

'Fit or no, there was nae ither for't,' replied Mrs Gillespie; '*somebody* maun be
bringing in whaur the faither hasna dune a
hand's turn sin Ne'erday. And it's no muckle
o' a wage I can mak' mysel wi' sae mony
things else adae.   A braw haunlin' o't I
hae, I can tell ye.'

'But don't your two great, strong girls
help you?   They should.'

'Help, said ye?' ejaculated Mrs Gillespie.
'Na, na; the haill place micht be tapsel-
teerie, an' no a finger o' ane o' them wad
wag to set it straicht.   Ower weariet when
they come in frae the wark, wi' their tale
o't.   But gin ony daffin's afit, they are sune
on the quievee—they'll rin like verra bleezes

then. In my time, folk wad pit through a
lang simmer day's field wark, or shearin' at
the hairst, an' think nocht o't; but *noo*—
keep me! it bates a wheen o' thae lasses to
lift a riddlefu' o' cauf!'

'The race degenerates,' responded Mrs
Brackenburn; 'every mother says so, but
they've got very low in the scale if they can't
so much as lift a riddle full of chaff. Your
husband has not been working since New
Year, you say. How is that?'

'You may ask! Sandy's the loopiest o'
the lot. Naething ever frae him but a leuk
an' a promise. A' thae days he has been
brisk at the curlin'—divertin' hissel' gran',
ye'll ken, but ne'er bringin' in a plack to keep
the kail-pat bilin' for the weans an' me. But
I *wull* be even wi' him the noo! He'll be
daunerin' hame or lang like a knotless threed,
seekin' his dinner. Weel, his dinner he'll
get, nae doot,—a hard, dry kin' o' bite, ye'll
see.'

The much-tried wife, as she ended speaking, pointed to a table in the farthest-away

corner; and, looking, the ladies perceived
that Alexander Gillespie's mid-day meal was
to consist of a pair of curling-stones.

Mrs Brackenburn's eyes danced. Ursula
was more struck than amused. Not a muscle
of the avenger's face relaxed from its wooden
immobility.

To save herself from laughing outright,
Mrs Brackenburn took refuge in a cough.

'Ye'll hae catch't a hoast, mem, I jalooze,'
observed Mrs Gillespie. 'Nae wunner, for
this hoose is as cauld as a lodge in a garden
o' cucumbers. It's between the deil an' the
deep sea here; a wide door or a smokin'
lum,—the tane or the tither.'

'Was that idea your own?' inquired Mrs
Brackenburn, with a struggle regaining her
gravity; 'or did you take it from the Border
family who used to do with a pair of spurs
what you have done with the curling-stones?'

'I ne'er heard tell o' nae sic folk,' said Mrs
Gillespie; 'but if they had a man in the
hoose like mine, they couldna but hae need
o' something to fricht him wi'.'

'Your way of frightening yours may be just,' said Mrs Brackenburn; 'I believe it is. But won't you be a little less severe? Think what a keen, sharp day it is, and how hungry your husband will be when he comes in.'

'He's ay that,' cried Mrs Gillespie feelingly. 'He comes na wi' the shovel but wi' the rake, him!'

Intercession was of no use; the offended matron would have her grim joke; so, after looking at the twins, and saying about them what people must say to mothers about babies, Mrs Brackenburn and Ursula rose to go. At the same moment Mrs Gillespie's husband crossed the threshold. On observing visitors, he precipitately retreated, believing himself to have been unnoticed. But his wife undeceived him by calling out satirically,—

'You're there, are ye? Ye needna aff an' awa' like a hunted peasweep; come ben an' gie the leddies a sicht o' a man that has been fleein' his dragon' (kite) 'ever sin' Ne'er-day.'

Alexander Gillespie disregarded the invitation. He seized a pair of wooden vessels which stood in the entry, cried back to his wife that he was going down to the well to fill her ' stoups ' for her, and escaped through the garden door, pursued by the ironical rejoinder,—

'That's richt; fill the stoups, Sandy; fill the stoups! cast a bane in the deil's teeth, if ye can.'

The next place to be visited was in the same row. Here, too, perfect cleanliness reigned; only here the appointments were pitifully scant; a deal table, two chairs, a bed, a grate, a clock—not a piece of art furniture, like that of Mrs Gillespie, but a mere ' wag-at-the-wa',—that was all. Three young children were rolling about on the faded carpet in the middle of the floor, and they were watched over by their grandmother, an almost helpless old woman, whose hands had been disjointed out of all semblance to hands by acute chronic rheumatism. Here was a fit object for commiseration, one would have supposed. But such she did not consider herself to be. Her mercies were so manifold, she said, that while at His own good time she would be ready to join the great congregation, she was meanwhile blithe to bide on a blink in the house of her pilgrimage. As for these children, whose father was dead, and whose mother was absent all day earning their livelihood and her own, 'The auld-farrant ways o' them is a fine divert, and aye keeps a body heartsome.'

'What a happy thing for you that you are so cheerful,' Mrs Brackenburn could not help saying.

'What would I be but cheerfu'?' was the reply. 'Providence is aye sae gran' to me.'

Very different was the succeeding scene. It was through a vennel where the houses were wretchedly tumble-down, up a rickety outside stair, in a miserable little room. The tenants were an old man and his wife. The man was so deaf that he invariably mistook what was said to him, and steadfastly persisted in assuming that every remark had reference in some way to 'baccy.'

The wife was loquacious—but with the unpleasantest loquacity. Her catalogue of grievances was as long as Don Giovanni's list of conquests; the parish did not attend to her; the clergy did not do their duty by her; the members of board were in league against her; the clothing society had refused to send a shawl to her; of the coals distributed by Baronshaugh, none had ever reached her. The curlers' meal? Oh, ay; a peck had been handed in; but of what use was that to one whose teeth refused oatcakes, and whose stomach did not lie to either porridge or cadgers' brose? But her chief injury, the one she dwelt upon longest, was the fact that, though in penury herself, she had rich relations in Netherlaw; her own brother's son was rolling in wealth, and driving his carriage.

'Geddes is the name o' him,' she said; '*Baillie* Geddes he ca's hissel for pride, but noucht o' a bailie was ever in't lang syne.

I kenna in what airt he has biggit his hoose,
but when ye gang through the toun ony
day, Mrs Brackenburn, ye micht tak a bit
leuk amang the terraces, and when ye fin'
oot Aunerach, pit him in mind that his
Auntie Leezie is in the laun o' the leevin'
yet.'

'I certainly think he ought to be reminded,' said Mrs Brackenburn. 'Should
you like him to be told that you weary to
see him ?'

'Nae need to say that,' responded the
crone. 'Tell him to sen' some siller, that's
a'. I am nane o' your wearyin' sort. I ha'e
ower muckle to tak up my heid.'

'And what does your head get taken up
with ?' asked Mrs Brackenburn.

'Wi' droll pliskies, whiles,' chuckled the
old woman. And as soon as her callers were
gone, she reverted to the mental pastime,
which their entrance had interrupted, thinking how she could best manage to pierce a
hole through the bottom of the rain-water
barrel of a neighbour who had offended her.

The following visit was to an Irish washer-
woman, who was so good a Catholic that
she crossed herself before holding any communication with heretics, and who always
kept twelve empty bobbins on her mantel-
piece, to represent the twelve apostles.

Then away from the vennel to the outer
rim of Laighbield, to speak comfortingly to
a dying woman ; then to see a bedridden
man ; after that, back to the main street
and into the post-office. Mrs Brackenburn
wished to procure a packet of pictorial cards
for her class, and Mr Mungo Mauchline,
illumined with smiles, appeared to serve her.
But soon he became overcast, for he could
not oblige his honoured customer to - day.
He had sent to Netherlaw for the 'kyards'
in question, but none had been forthcoming.

'From wheech I conclude,' quoth he, 'that
either the second edeetion has been referred,
or else that the author has stopped ushering
them.   Which is undoubtedly to be regretted, for these kyards were, I oun, the
neatest thing I have yet beheld in the way

of a multymipaavy' (*multum in parvo*, he was supposed to mean) 'of use and beauty, —oh dear, yes.' And with this, Mr Mungo Mauchline grew happy again.

Having heard of Mrs Brackenburn's present doings (Mrs Brackenburn had little chance in Laighbield of doing deeds, either good or bad, by stealth), he took occasion to throw in his word of commendation and encouragement.

'Ondiscreeminate charity is a bane, ma'am,' he exclaimed ;—'a perfec' burlyskew ; but yours and this young lady's, that is a different storry—that is a boundless blessing.'

And he thereupon became inspired with matter for a song ; so that an ode was penned within the hour, in which Mrs Brackenburn was described as—

'The welcome messenger of Day,
Who, what time she goes into the poor man's house,
Does of her purse make a proud, rich display.'

As the ladies were leaving the post-office, a young minister, somewhat of a clerical dandy, passed by, and with studied grace made obeisance to Mrs Brackenburn.

'Our U.P. brother,' said she to her friend.

'And what of him?' was the careless rejoinder.

'Stage-struck when a boy,' drawled Mrs Brackenburn; 'speaks English mincingly, and French with the Netherlaw accent; pulpit style,—"Who knows what strange, mysterious tale the wild wind whispers to the trembling leaf?"'

This caused Ursula to look so serious that her companion inquired what the matter was. She did not say, and the question was repeated. They were at the moment going through the narrow, wood-walled passage of one of the closes in the Wynd, and at the reiteration Ursula stood still. Taking Mrs Brackenburn by the hands, she said, in a low tone,—

'Matilda, you pick people to pieces so mercilessly, — you so hold everything and everybody up to ridicule,—your criticism is so unsparing,—that if I did not love, I am afraid I should hate you.'

Mrs Brackenburn gravely bowed her acknowledgments.

'I would rather be loved by a few, and hated by the rest, than liked indifferently well by all,' she declared, and airily led the way up the steep and winding wooden staircase. Up—up—up, till they reached a garret. It was curtained with bright chintz, and it was carpeted. It contained, besides essentials, a mahogany chest of drawers, polished to mirror-like clearness, and covered on the top with a white mat, on which were set a looking-glass, a few books, and a case of stuffed foreign birds ; there was a cupboard too, as lustrous as the drawers, with glass-door to the upper half, displaying the gay-coloured, old-fashioned 'tea-set' within. The windows were blinded ; and in the recess in the wall, which was fitted up as a bed, a woman lay, worn and pale, but most delicately clean. 'She was gey an' dowie ways,' she said, in answer to inquiries. She had not been able

to do anything all day—not even to kindle
her fire in the morning.

'But I'm thinking,' she added, with a faint
smile, 'it's as weel, when I am off work, to
ha'e the day's coal hained.'

'Without a fire in this miserably cold
weather!' exclaimed Mrs Brackenburn. 'It
is terrible to think of. And has no one been
near you all day, Christina?'

'The wee things frae below cam' an'
chappit whiles, but couldna rax up to un-
steek the sneck, so had aye just to rin awa'
doon,' she replied.

'When you are ill, and Dr Brackenburn
tells me that you often are, you ought not to
be alone. Surely some friend would stay
with you.'

'I canna burden strangers,' said the woman,
'and I ha'e nane o' my ain noo. But I am
used wi' lanesomeness, and dinna tak so ill
wi't as you might think.'

Mrs Brackenburn's opinion was that, were
she herself in such case, she would far rather
die at once than live on in a world so

desolate. But she did not spend time in sentimentalising ; she drew her gloves off, and, in spite of the sick woman's horrified remonstrance at sight of a 'denty leddy fyling her fingers,' found out where the fuel was kept, and proceeded to kindle the fire.

' I know very well how to make a fire,' she said, as she put sticks and coals into the grate. ' I have done it scores of times in the woods, for gipsy tea.'

And she did not go until she had seen the room looking comfortable and cheery in the flame-light.

Christina had protested that she *could* not touch any food to-day ; but something would presently be sent from the manse that would surely tempt her from her fasting. Meantime Mrs Brackenburn called Ursula to halt at the first door down stairs.

The mistress of the household was Mrs George Choppin, she, you may recollect, whose husband was celebrated for upholding his 'door cheeks.' Several women were in the kitchen (which, by the way, was none of the tidiest), knitting bonnets and gossiping full briskly. Some children, newly home from school, were dining at a small, round table in the background,—the bill of fare, sheep's feet and potatoes with the coats on. The dinner service was not very extensive; no table-linen, nor even knives, forks, or plates. Each child simply held a 'trotter' in one hand and a potato in the other.

Mrs Brackenburn's account of matters overhead was received with quite a chorus of comment.

'Did ever ye!' exclaimed one.

'If she had as muckle to dae as a wheen o' us, she wadna' ha'e nae time for nervishness and dwaums,' said Mrs Choppin.

'Kirsty Kerr's ower prood and independent,' cried a third—'*that's* what she's! She'll no loot to let on that she's needfu' o' help; it's a' her ain wyte she's no leukit tae.'

'That's true,' put in another. 'A cairt o' Baronshaugh's coals was broucht till her— an' she canna be oot o' the want o' them—

but what does Kirsty dae but sen' them straicht back. She hadna come to that o't yet; she could work for her ain coals, quo' she. It was her great-granny, as I ha'e heard my mither tell, wha, when umbrellas first cam in fashion hereawa, wadna thole nae siccan toy to cross *her* doorstep, for she thoucht it baith sin an' shame to haud the guid rain o' heaven aff ye. And Kirsty has a' the auld ane's dourness, whatever mair forby.'

'Christina Kerr is a good, brave, independent woman,' said Mrs Brackenburn, in a tone which made the click of the knitting-needles cease. 'If all of you would follow her example, instead of finding fault with her, Laighbield would profit by the change.'

This was true enough, only the saying of it was not the way by which a minister's wife might hope to increase her popularity.

The sick woman having been commended to neighbourly attention, the day's visiting was done, and Mrs Brackenburn and Ursula left the Wynd. Walking towards the manse they

could see, away among the crisp-white fields
in the distance, the Laighbield curling pond.
Stones were skimming the ice, besoms sweep-
ing, and players roaring amain.   Another
match was in progress, having as its end
meal for the poor.   The design of thus feed-
ing the hungry was laudable—no doubt of
that ; but, unfortunately, some of these charitable curlers, like Alexander Gillespie, forgot
where all true charity must begin.

CHAPTER IV.

IN 'THE BARONSHAUGH LAFT.'

'Twice holy was the Sabbath bell :
The silent streets were crowded well
With staid and pious companies,
Warm from their fireside orat'ries.'

'AN instrumental performance !—a *voluntary!* We shall have rubric and surplice next.'

The speaker, as you guess, was Mrs Cassillis of Baronshaugh, who had met Miss Elvester and her girls at the churchyard gates, while the bell was ringing for morning service.

'Excuse me,' said Miss Elvester, 'but I fail to see the connection.'

'The thin end of the wedge, the first

letting in of water,' replied Mrs Cassillis, with
a delicious confusion of metaphor not unfre-
quent in her conversation. 'Instrumental
music now' (Mrs Brackenburn had lately
presented an organ to the parish church);
'presently choristers, to turn the grave, sweet
melody commanded by the Psalmist into a
concert to minister to vain imaginations, and
in due time a service not unlike the Romish
celebration of the mass : blade—ear—full
corn in the ear.'

Through the gaps in his mother's oration,
the feebler tones of the young laird were
heard. He wanted to know if Ulrica were
still pleased with the Baronshaugh Gallery;
and if she would come to the Free Church
for a change, some day ?

'Not an altogether unwholesome change,
I believe,' said his mother approvingly; 'and
should either Miss Elvester or any of her
sisters think of trying it, I shall be most
happy to accommodate them.'

Miss Elvester, on her own and sisters'
behalf, acknowledged the obliging offer; and

Mrs Cassillis proceeded to say, addressing herself to Christian,—

'I am well aware that the old landmarks have been removed, and that the leeks and garlic of what is called "preaching to the times" are more palatable to the rising generation than the pure manner of doctrinal teaching; still, I invite you to give the unvarnished preaching of the Word a trial. This is your last Sabbath here; I know what husks are presented to you as spiritual food where you worship at Netherlaw; come with me to-day, and for once avail yourself of the privilege of a sound gospel discourse.'

All the more that it was her last Sunday here, did Christian object to spend it, or any part of it, with Mrs Cassillis. Yet how ex cuse herself? Hardly by saying plainly what was the truth, that she was not willing to put herself under the influence of that 'sound gospel discourse.' Would not Jenny interpose to save her? and she looked appealingly at her sister to that end. In vain. There was amusement mingled with mischief

in Miss Elvester's grey eyes; but she would
not interfere.   Christian was independent
now, and among the pleasures of independence ranked that of saying yes or no for
one's-self.   Since her sister would not speak,
then, Christian must.

'This is our last day together; should you
mind my leaving you, Jenny?' she asked;
and her upturned face added plainly, 'Do
bid me stay.'

'Not a whit!' said Miss Elvester, smiling
on her.   'Go with Mrs Cassillis, my dear,
and I shall be extremely glad if you hear a
better gospel than Dr Brackenburn could
preach to you.'

The answering glance was full of reproach,
and on Mrs Cassillis remarking that, 'naturally she took an interest in the spiritual
well-being of Miss Christian Elvester,' Christian ungratefully thought that the indifference
of the lady of Baronshaugh would be vastly
more convenient than the interest of her was.

The laird being now discovered telling
Ulrica that he did not curl nor skate,—there

were often accidents on the ice, and if you
get wet it made you feel very damp and '—
was pounced upon by his stern parent, while
he paused, seeking for words to express
what else besides very damp it made you
feel, and solemnly reminded of the Fourth
Commandment.

Yet, next moment, Mrs Cassillis observed,
as a pretty fashionably-dressed girl entered
the gates,—

'There goes the young person who is
engaged to your friend, the parish minister
of Auchterbrechan ; and no doubt Langbiggin, her uncle, has made her a prize well
worth Mr Donald Berwick's grasping at.
Langbiggin is one of our elders. I must
speak to him about allowing the girl to
flaunt herself in the Established Church !
That will let him see how much respect I
can have for the principles of a Free
Church elder, who countenances the engagement of his niece to a minister of the
Establishment.'

And this surely was talk as secular as that

about curling and skating and accidents on
the ice.

'Come, Miss Christian Elvester,' said the
lady peremptorily, as Christian was casting
a lingering look after the multitude, 'you
shall worship for one day of your life in the
Free Church, instead of in the House of
Bondage;' and then, having in this high-
handed manner taken possession, she told
her captive that a special collection was to be
lifted to-day on behalf of the evangelisation
of the Highlands and Islands. She spoke
much louder than she need have done, and
with intent; the train of townspeople passing into the House of Bondage might hear,
and consider, and feel rebuked; for it was
well known that the Established Church was
shamefully remiss in the matter of making
a collection.

Laighbield parish kirk had no pretensions
to beauty; the steeple was too thick for its
length, and the belfry too small for the
general bulk of the building; the windows
should have been larger, and the doors might

with advantage have been wider. Neither
were the surroundings to be boasted of.
There were no yews and cypresses, no
flower-railed enclosures, no tomb-gardens
here. This burying place was grassy all
over, and instead of graceful obelisks, broken
columns, and marble urns, you had moss-
grown slabs, and death's-heads, and cross-
bones, and cherubs most woefully defaced by
years and weather.

A dark spiral staircase at the back of the
church led to what was known in local par-
lance as 'The Baronshaugh Laft.' This was
the only gallery, and it bore the Cassillis
coat-of-arms on its oak panneling. The
family pew was fitted up with crimson cur-
tains and ancient chairs, high-backed and
elaborately carved. Behind were the servants' sittings—unused now, for since the
death of the late laird Mrs Cassillis would
only employ domestics of her own persuasion
on church government; so here Mrs Brackenburn had found a place for her organ.

Everybody who could see the gallery stared

up at it when the Elvesters appeared. That
was Laighbield manners.   The young women
might get hints in millinery and deportment
there.   The manse pew had long been their
fashion-place, but the 'Baronshaugh Laft' had
of late made a pleasing variety ; so from week
to week the note-taking was practised with
perfectly frank obviousness.

To-day Ursula faced the scrutiny with a
colder, prouder air than usual.   Only a
minute ago she had heard something which
moved her considerably, and the more Ursula
was ruffled inwardly, the more haughty she
would outwardly appear.

The pulpit, which faced the gallery, was
still unoccupied ; but yonder, in the manse-
pew, sat Mrs Brackenburn, and beside her
smiled Miss Langbiggin, the Rev. Donald
Berwick's second niece.   So sweetly pretty
she was, too !—so in every way suited to be
a clergyman's wife.   What could the rejected
suitor have done better ?   Had Ursula not
bidden him forget her and seek some fitter
bride ?   Should she not then be glad to learn

that he had so speedily obeyed? And she *would* be glad of it. Oh yes, by-and-by, when the thought had become familiar, she would certainly be glad of it. In the meanwhile she mechanically opened her Bible, and read some verses several times over without having an idea what they were about.

How she hated herself for this weakness, so unreasoning — so pitiful! But service would commence immediately, and she would get into a better frame. Dr Brackenburn's grave, sympathetic voice had always a tranquillising charm with it, and—

Her senses were scattered suddenly by a voice which, instead of tranquillising her, caused her to tremble violently, while the hot blood rushed to her face, then back again, leaving her paler than before; for during the moments she had been looking at these uncomprehended verses, Donald Berwick had ascended the pulpit.

She rose with the rest of the congregation when they stood up to sing, and looked intently at her open psalter; but anybody

glancing over her shoulder would have made
the discovery that the book was held upside
down. Poor Ursula! she had of late been
struggling so hard to banish everything connected with her past life from memory, and
to live entirely in Laighbield and the present.
And this was the measure of her success—this!

The idea of leaving the church presented
itself to her ; but she had presence of mind
enough left to remember that to do so would
be owning to Jenny what she never—either
to Jenny or to any other—would own. So
she stayed still, and heard Mr Berwick
preach ; and he, if he looked at her at all,
would notice only that she seemed the most
impassive, most uninterested of his auditors.

When all was over, the Elvesters found
Mrs Brackenburn sauntering in the churchyard, waiting for them. She was in a perfect glow of self-renouncing ardour, she
declared. The sermon had gone to her
conscience.

'You instinctively tell when a man is
speaking from the heart, and when only

from the ear,' said she, 'and Mr Berwick
spoke from the heart to-day. Yes; before
teaching it to others, he must have himself
learnt the duty of refusing to sink into a
sullen grumbler when things do not go as
one wants, and of breaking through the
narrow limits of self, rising by suffering
into fuller sympathy with one's kind. But
I wonder what pleasant thing he has ever
longed for and had denied him. It is no
business of mine, however; and, at any
rate, he has as many pleasant things now as
ought to satisfy him—though, indeed, he was
not looking quite so sunny as such a fortunate man should when I bade him and Miss
Langbiggin good-bye a minute ago. He
is staying with Miss Berwick at the Neuk,
so his way and Katie Langbiggin's lie together.'

Miss Elvester did not make any remark
about Mr Berwick's way and Miss Langbiggin's being likely to lie together through
life. She had heard of that arrangement
even before to-day; Christian had told the

news to her, but neither she nor Christian had thought it necessary to mention the matter to Ursula.

'Even the old farmers went to sleep with one ear open to-day,' continued Mrs Brackenburn. 'And there was not nearly so much wondering on the mountains of vanity as usual; was there, Ursula?'

'Why not?' returned Ursula; 'for who could wander over mountains of vanity while Dr Brackenburn preaches?'

'I both can and do,' said Dr Brackenburn's wife. 'And I'm not sure about you either. I daresay you are no better than the weaver who felt so positive as to the fixedness of his thoughts during sermon, that he took a wager on the subject. (My husband says I am as bad as Mr Mungo Mauchline with my "stories;" but bear with me.) On the Sunday after the bet, the preacher had hardly begun when that weaver caught himself calculating how many looms might be set up in the area of the church. And you, Ursula, don't you think that if you were to watch closely you might surprise yourself counting the tulips on Mrs Gillespie's bonnet, or wishing that somebody would kindly tell John Craig, of Scroggiehillock, how much to one side his wig is, or wondering if the sleeper near you won't hit the book-board with his nose next time he nods? This morning, attentive as I plume myself upon having been, I yet once lost the thread, thinking how becomingly Mr Berwick's chesnut hair curved itself about his square forehead, and what fine hazel eyes he had; and another time I missed what he was saying, while I informed myself that, with all his good looks, there wasn't one touch of the ladies' pet parson about him. But I suspect your wanderings would take a different direction, for it seems to me that Mr Berwick is no favourite of yours. Am I right, Miss Elvester?'

'Not to my knowledge,' said Miss Elvester, laughing it off. 'I have brought up my girls well, I hope, and I never allow them to say anything disrespectful of the clergy.'

'One of your girls is missing, I see. Does she worship to-day in the temple of immensity?'

'No, but with Mrs Cassillis of Baronshaugh.'

'Unhappy Christian! for she has been borne off against her will, no doubt, to hear "that blessed word Messopotamia."'

While her elders talked, Ulrica instructed herself among the tombs. And when Mrs Brackenburn had taken leave of the others, she found the child standing at the side of the church, gazing thoughtfully at a strong leather strap, like a dog's collar, suspended from the wall by a short iron chain.

'I have often wanted to know what that is,' said Ursula, 'but Jenny won't explain. She is so provoking sometimes; indeed, you haven't any notion how she suppresses one's mind.'

'As Chinese ladies suppress their girls' feet, is it?'

'Yes; and the mind is of far more importance than the feet. Please do you tell

me what that is—please do. Jenny calls it
a relic of the dark ages.'

'I will have Miss Elvester excommuni-
cated, if she dares to call anything belong-
ing to Laighbield Kirk by such a naughty
name. What that is? It is " the jougs."
Long ago, you must know, when people
didn't behave prettily, they were not left to
their own consciences—perhaps they hadn't
got any in those days; at any rate, they were
first " dealt with " by the session, and then
brought here and chained to the church wall
during the pleasure of their judges.'

Ulrica's eyes dilated.

'I almost never know whether you are in
earnest, or whether you are only joking,' she
said.

'I am in earnest now—in dead earnest;
one never jokes on Sunday.'

'Then I wish I had not asked about that
horrible, horrible thing,' said Ulrica, slowly.
'I shall never be able to put it out of my
mind, never again; and I so *hate* to think
of it.'

Hearing this, Mrs Brackenburn became very angry with herself, and felt as one feels who has unwittingly done a mischief to some delicate piece of mechanism. She tried to efface the impression of these thoughtless words of hers. To no purpose: Ulrica scarcely seemed to hear; Ulrica had been beyond measure shocked, and she would be miserable, as only sensitive children can be miserable, for the rest of the day.

CHAPTER V.

MRS BRACKENBURN'S TRIBULATIONS.

> Thus roll I, never taking ease
> My tub, like Saint Diogenes,
> Now serious am, now seek to please ;
> Now love and hate in twin, one sees
> The motives now are those, now these ;
> Now nothings now realities.
> Thus roll I, never taking ease,
> My tub, like Saint Diogenes.

THE study in Laighbield manse was the veritable workshop of a labourer ; yet there caught the eye, here and yonder, amidst the literary profusion, such incongruities as a lace handkerchief, or a tiny silver thimble. Mrs Brackenburn had no business to leave these properties about the room, but then she did not think that her husband had the least objection to see them there.

He must surely have objected, however, to a rustle — rustle — rustle of silken garments, which, on the occasion now chronicled, prevented him from concentrating his attention on the subject he had in hand. Added to this distracting sound, too, was the consciousness that she who caused it was counting the moments till she should have freedom of speech accorded her. At length the writer laid down his pen, left the philosophers whose theories he was reviewing only half discussed, shifted his position from the desk to the fireside, and bade his wife come talk to him.

Nothing loath was she. Having seated herself on a footstool close to his chair, she said,—

' You see beside you a woman with a whole chapter of tribulations on her mind. What would you advise : to bear in silence, or to recapitulate ? '

'In her case to recapitulate might be the better plan, I think.'

'Ah! it is as well you counsel so. I should be sure to recapitulate, at any rate. I asked advice, but meant to follow it only if it went with my own inclination.'

'So I imagine. *I* find that seekers of advice generally, though not so candid as you in avowing it, are pretty much of your way of thinking.'

'To be sure they are; if your advice points in the direction they incline to, that is charming, for they can go on all the more joyfully; but if in the opposite way, why, they'll thank you, and—let it alone. When I have not really known which of two things I wished to do, I have sometimes, instead of asking advice, tossed a penny. That always settled the question; for I immediately wanted to do just the reverse of what the penny had decided for me. But now for my tribulations, Alan. The first is, that nature should have behaved so unhandsomely towards me that I can be called "the unbrawest wee wife ever

a man waled for himself." I heard a woman
(they have such voices, those Laighbieldists!)
say so to one of my servants to-day.'

'You do not mean to tell me that such a
remark as that troubled you!'

'Oh, it troubled me immensely, and it has
sent me to you to ask if I am really so bad as
they call me. Am I?'

'I could give you my opinion, of course;
have I not been again and again assured that
it is of no value on such points.?

'You are the most unsatisfactory man on
earth, Dr Brackenburn; there is no possibility
of wringing, or beguiling, or surprising a compliment from you. Even while you were my
lover, and ought to have had a glamour over
you, you never ceased to think me plain and
insignificant to the last degree.'

'Was it not, then, all the more flattering
that I should have been your lover notwithstanding?'

'Perhaps, still, and just for the novelty,
I should have liked one man in the world
blindly to think me fair. Well, you know,

my first tribulation; console me, can't you—
console me! No, no; not in that way' (for
he was treating her as one would a child that
had come to one for comfort). 'But such
was ever your plan — caresses in place of
compliments.'

'The next tribulation, Matilda?'

'You are the source of my next—yes, you!
and for this—you are hypercritical in regard
to my conduct, yet you never give so much
as one thought to my mode of hairdressing.
Now, I am rather proud of my hair (don't
grudge me the small vanity, it is my only
one!), and it is mortifying to find that
you take no interest in it; that I may walk
before you a whole day, wearing it exactly
as Mrs Inverarity wears hers, and you will
never perceive the change.'

'I did fancy that there was a something
unusual about your appearance to-day. And
it is the hairdressing, is it? Let me look at
it rightly, now,' and he held her at arm's
length for the purpose.

The hair had been drawn back from the

face and up from the neck, and made as
little of as possible, and tightly gathered into
a twist behind the ears; in fact, everything
had been done to render it as unbecoming as
such very pretty hair could be rendered.

'You did observe that I looked unusual,'
she cried, laughingly, as he scanned her;
'you did come to the conclusion that I was
even less lovely than my wont. How gratify-
ing! Say, though, does my reverend critic
like the style?'

'I can't pretend that I do.'

'Why? It is beautifully, smoothly, glossily
tidy—not one lock astray—every scrap of
brow I've got displayed. Why, do you not
like it?'

'Because it does not content the eye.
When it is in soft folds—'

'Folds! Alan; folds of hair!'

'I don't know your toilet technicalities.'

'You don't know a hair-pin from a darn-
ing-needle.'

'When it is arranged as you wear it
usually, the effect is that one is constantly

tempted to stroke it. Will that serve as a compliment, my dear?'

'By no means; it only serves to show me what value I may set on your endearments.'

Saying which, Mrs Brackenburn crossed the rug and seated herself in an opposite easy-chair.

'Another tribulation is,' she said, 'the near prospect of a visit from my forty-second cousin, Dugald Urquhart. He is at Barons-haugh now, and will be here immediately; and the thought is bitter to me.'

'I am surprised to hear you—you who are so hospitable.'

'There are exceptions to every rule—if you will excuse me for treating you to a slightly threadbare piece of information— and my exception is Mr Urquhart—I know very well why he is coming here; he thinks it will sound impressive to say to his friends, "You have heard of Brackenburn of Laigh-bield—the scholar and critic? His wife is a cousin of mine, and I have just been stay-ing with them. Brackenburn is a fine fellow" (no, he wont say " fine fellow ; " his style is too stilted for that)—" is a man of great parts. He and I had many most interesting discussions ; and some of them, I flatter myself, will have their reflection on his next contribution to literature." '

' My dear Matilda, you have the most remarkable habit of furnishing absent persons with ideas and speeches, and then of judging as if these were really theirs and not your own. It is all very well to give your characterizations a dramatic cast, but certainly not so well to condemn people for thoughts which you only imagine them to think, and words which have never been spoken, saving by yourself.'

' I have made a special study of Dugald Urquhart, Alan ; I have sometimes amused myself by considering what he would say if such and such a remark were made to him ; then I have experimented, and received a reply as nearly as possible what I looked for. Oh, he is shallow as a summer brook, though he makes believe to be deep as the sea where

it can't be sounded. Yes ; I understand that
simile, Dr Brackenburn ; it means that I of
all people ought to have patience with
shallowness. But I am not finding fault
with shallowness—we are not responsible for
our mental capacity any more than we are for
the cast of our features ; what I rail against
is the affection of depth. To hear Dugald
discourse grandly on art, for instance, always
makes me long to exclaim aloud, " Shak-
speare and the musical glasses."'

'Is it quite fair to measure by your own
knowledge of art, how much or how little
your cousin knows about it ? '

' Pardon me, pardon me, I do not measure
so ; but I know the difference between sham
and reality. Mr Urquhart has been about a
good deal, and has picked up the common-
places of artists and the like, and can echo
them glibly enough ; but it is all empty
sound. He will talk about spending hours
of rapture in the art galleries of Europe ; but
come to particulars, and not the ghost of a
perception does he convey to you of all the

glory and the greatness. Just once walk with
him through any collection of paintings, hear
his stereotyped praise of whatever it is the
fashion to speak well of, and notice how he
passes over all else with a remark flung
chancewise, that this is " badly grouped,"
and that wants unity, and the other has been
" conventionally handled ; " after such a walk
you won't have much belief in his artistic
instincts left.   Poetry is Dugald's speciality ;
yet whenever I have asked him to interpret
anything too high for me, he has found that
it would be very difficult to get a lady to
take hold of the meaning ; and so it would
be, if the man who was to explain it hadn't
taken hold himself.   But there is one redeeming point about my cousin Dugald—he
never, never makes a joke.   I have often
been glad of that, because if he *were* seized
with a desire to be funny, I know what he
would do.   He would make a round of all
the circuses in the kingdom, taking notes of
the conversation of clowns.   Now, do you
pant for closer communion with the man ? '

'Certainly not with the man as you have painted him. But suppose the case is reversed : suppose I knew little or nothing of Mr Urquhart's cousin Matilda, but was on terms of intimacy with Mr Urquhart himself, and suppose he should one day sketch the lady for my better information ; might it not be that I would not pant for closer communion with her, so sketched ?'

'I am positive you would not, for the sketch would be appalling. Dugald thinks that a woman who can give an answer back, and who asks, "What is the meaning ?" when you use phrases you have no right to, is the most unpardonable blunder in the universe. He and I can never be in harmony. I am in the key of six sharps, I suppose, while he is in five flats, and we jar accordingly. We have a demoralising influence on each other.'

'Then decidedly he had better not come here.'

'But he *will* come here. He and his sister have the most delightfully frank way of requiring no invitation to the houses of people to whom they are bound by the ties of kindred or affection, as Mr Carnegy would say. Well, now that I've abused the young man to my heart's content, I feel much better—I shall be able to receive him with at least surface civility. You need have no fear about me, Alan ; I shall not forget what is due to a guest, as I once might if the guest had sorely tempted me to it. Surely I improve; surely I may soon be thinking of setting up a diary.'

'My wife's diary will be a curiosity in literature.'

'As much a curiosity, I daresay, as the copy-books of my boys are, which reminds me of what I had nearly forgotten, the heaviest of all my tribulations. I have been praising myself, have I ? but now I must let myself down again, for I am weary in well-doing ; *so* weary, alas !'

'I am sorry for that. What is the discouragement ?'

'Those children make no progress. For weeks I have laboured to get in some faint

dawn of grammar and common sense upon
their minds; for I don't confine myself to
either altogether, you know. I almost think
they could tell the difference now between noun
and verb, further I would not dare to vouch
for them. I was vain enough to cultivate
hopes about the adjective also, but to-night
these hopes were blighted utterly; for on my
putting the question, " In what degree of
comparison is " Larger?" one boy hesitat-
ingly suggested, " Femiline," and another
improved upon the idea by boldly shouting
" Masculum;" and all the rest were blank.
It sounds comic, doesn't it? Yet it is very
sober earnest to me.'

' I have not a doubt of that, nor any
wonder at your weariness. But, my love, no
work is without its discouragements, and the
work best worth doing has generally the
largest share of these. Workers, however,
are all the stronger for having bravely met
and overcome the obstacles and difficulties
by which they are withstood. And do not
think, Matilda, that your labour has been

lost, even though your boys cannot yet com-
pare the adjective. As a proof to the con-
trary, I have several times been asked if I
could not induce you to open a second class
—one for girls.'

'Perish the thought!—I mean I would
rather shut up the class I have now than
open another. I know the extreme sketchi-
ness of female education in Laighbield—how
the women for the most part read with difficulty and write with distress ; but don't, so
please you, don't give the task of reform to
me, who am overweighted as it is.'

'Could Miss Ursula Elvester, do you suppose, be persuaded to take up the matter ?'

'My princess among the bonnet girls!'

'And why not?   It would do your
princess a vast deal of lasting good, if she
could be roused out of her high-flown, senti-
mental day-dreaming, and got to take a
healthy interest in her fellow-creatures.'

'Why so severe? Does it mean that you
do not like Ursula ?'

'Rather it means that I do like her, and

see in her the possibility of much good. In teaching those girls, the young lady would herself learn more than she at present has any conception of. And if she would but try to make brighter the lives of those about her, she would at the same time greatly brighten her own. Do you not think that a woman's truest happiness lies in making the people around her happy ?'

'So men tell us. But I've a feeling that it is a roundabout sort of route to happiness, whereas I would have a shorter for Princess Ursula. I want to see her married.'

'Matilda! Matilda!'

'Yes, Dr Brackenburn ; and more than that, I have a husband for her in view—a very fine young man, dear—my cousin Jack.'

'That is what has caused your sudden access of affection for Jack, and your insistance upon his paying a visit to Laighbield, whether he will or no.'

'Exactly. And I tell you of it now, so that when he comes you may not be a hindrance to me ; for, unless a man gets

warned off beforehand, he is fatally sure to
make a great rent right through any artful
little web his wife may be quietly weaving.
Don't shake your head though ; there is no
harm in this, but good only.   I have the
interest of those young persons warmly at
heart, and I am convinced that it is not well
for either of them to be alone.   When I am
dead and gone, dear, and you give memorials
of me to the world, don't forget to say that I
ever found my truest happiness in making
others happy.   Heigho ! would anybody
believe you if you did say that, I wonder ?
Shall you wear my ring, then, to keep me in
remembrance, Alan ?   It must be enlarged
first, for, as it is, it would barely pass the
tips of your finger.   Let me try.'

She drew off her wedding-ring for the
purpose, and went back to her husband's
side.   Dr Brackenburn would not let her
carry her intention into effect.   He took the
ring and replaced it on its proper finger,
and—well, there was no more talk of dying
that night.

CHAPTER VI.

LITERARY CRITICISMS.

'We need all the counter-weights we can muster to
balancet he sad realities of life. God has made
sunny spots in the heart ; why should we exclude
the light from them ?'

THE parish church clock was striking
nine. A keen March wind—'a
rantin', tantin', tearin' wind,' as the
minister in Mr Mungo Mauchline's 'storry'
said—was searching Laighbield for people to
persecute. Ten or a dozen girls came from
a close in the Wynd, and having screened
themselves in their plaids, and exchanged a
few parting pleasantries, took their several
ways home.

That was Ursula's class. Surprising, is it ?

But Ursula was devoted to duty, it must be
remembered; and even so far as this had
her devotion led her.   Until now, it must
be owned, she had not entered very heartily
into the spirit of her work.   She was new to
such labours, and there had been many trials
to damp, but never a triumph to cheer her;
for the material she had in hand was un-
shapely, and it was anything but plastic.

On this present cold March night, our
young social reformers felt particularly de-
pressed and tired, so much so, that it became
a question whether she would not go straight
home rather than follow her usual custom
after teaching, of spending the remainder of
the evening at the manse.   She had not seen
Mrs Brackenburn for a week, though; so,
after all, habit prevailed, and to the manse
she went.   Being on no ceremony there, she
did not summon a servant to admit her, but
finding the outer door already open, opened
the inner glass-door for herself, left her wraps
in the proper place, and proceeded to the
drawing-room.

Ursula was sorry immediately that she had not yielded to her first impulse, and gone home—second thoughts were not always best, it seemed. For her friend was not alone as she had expected to find her. Standing beside Mrs Brackenburn, gaily laughing and talking with her, was the man who, of all people in the world, Ursula Elvester was least prepared to meet—the minister of Auchterbrechan. Near these two a young lady, correctly pretty, and in every particular very much according to rule, was being entertained by a young man bearing a decided resemblance to Mrs Brackenburn — these were Miss Langbiggin and the cousin Jack, whom Mrs Brackenburn designed for Princess Ursula. Cousin Jack had arrived to-day. There was also present another arrival of to-day, the more distant cousin, Dugald; and he was looking over lithographs, marvelling the while, in that superior way of his, how any man calling himself an intelligent being could possibly take an interest in Matilda Brackenburn's chatter.

At the last meeting of Ursula Elvester
and Donald Berwick, nine months ago, she
had been cold and self-possessed, he—the girl
had sometimes trembled since, thinking of
it—terribly impassioned.   Now parts were
changed; he might never have cared a rush
about her, for anything his manner showed,
while she—oh, she was vexed with herself
for this weak and foolish flutter!   But, just
as that day in church, she was more concerned
on the score of appearances than she need
have been; the flutter she was so ashamed
of was not on the surface; any bystander
would merely have noticed that Ursula looked
proudly reserved, and would have inferred
that this was because she shrank from meeting with one who had known her in better
days.   Half-a-minute and the ordeal was
over—the pair, who might to-day have been
husband and wife, had touched hands, asked
each other ceremoniously how they did, and
fallen apart again,—she manifestly relieved,
he with something in his style which Mrs
Brackenburn could not make out — was

it dislike? or was it only an excess of indifference?

Strange to tell, Dugald Urquhart's fancy was taken at first sight by the queenly girl, whose garments were indebted to her for their air of distinction, not she to them for hers, and who had obviously the good sense to remember that this popular preacher—this encourager of Matilda Brackenburn's empty puerilities, was only a son of the soil when all was said. Besides this, Ursula had far more presence than her sister Christian; she was statuesquely beautiful in the manner of —Mr Urquhart forgot what statue exactly it was, but that to be sure was neither here nor there. Under the mellow influence of this sudden admiration, Dugald reversed his usual tactics. In place of assuming the defensive, he lay in wait for Ursula, lured her to the table where he had been solitarily feasting his eye, and, not taking thought that she was far less a stranger in the manse than himself, proceeded to act as exponent of all the albums.

Mrs Brackenburn's cousin Jack asked Miss Langbiggin if *she* liked to look at albums; and Miss Langbiggin replied that she liked to look at albums very much indeed. But had the question been, did she like to hear discussions on politics, or to make wax flowers, or to listen to the music of the future, the young lady's answer would have been just the same.

'I wonder if there is an album of horrors among that lot,' said cousin Jack. 'The Marionette (my cousin, I mean, she was brought up with us, and we fellows called her nothing but the Marionette) used to rejoice in such a treasure. Once when Dr Brackenburn was at our place, long before there was any thought of his marriage it was, my cousin forgetfully introduced her album of horrors by name to him. He opened it up, and, "the first horror I see here is myself," he said. I suppose Mr Brackenburn now-a-days keeps clear of scrapes like that. She'll be just a little bit unpopular, else.'

Miss Langbiggin smiled a small, neat smile, and rejoined that Mrs Brackenburn was very much liked by everybody in Laighbield, which was a slight deviation from fact; but it *is* difficult, when one thinks of it, to keep ever straight along the narrow track of truthfulness, swerving neither to the right hand nor the left.

Mrs Brackenburn now bespoke her cousin's attention.

'Do you remember a game called Literary Criticism which we used to play at long ago?' she asked.

Yes; he accurately remembered.

'Well, games generally help a company to amalgamate; so we're going to have Literary Criticism now. *Ergo*, you will go to the study, paper and pencil-hunting, if you please.'

'And have your husband presently turn me out into the night for meddling with his things,' demurred Jack.

'No, my cousin; even if you should upset an inkstand or so; Dr Brackenburn will only sigh and say, " Oh, Diamond, Diamond, thou little knowest the mischief thou hast done !"   Come, Katie; we are going to make a literary woman of you—you are to review a book.'

Miss Langbiggin rose at once and took her place at the table, round which Donald Berwick was arranging seats.   Jack departed for material.

Neither of the remaining pair was so complaisant; neither of them seemed to see the necessity for the amalgamation which Mrs Brackenburn desired.

'I could not write anything like that,' Ursula said, when the thing was explained to her.   'I have neither invention nor originality.'

'Capital!' thought Mr Urquhart; 'this is the proper womanly spirit.   *She* would not presumptuously tell a man that his verses were only fit for the Poet's Corner in the *Cornrigshire Chronicler.*'

The gentleman's own reason for withholding from Literary Criticism was not

lack of invention and originality. No;
but—

'In my humble opinion, labour of the
pen is too lofty to be made the butt of
idle travesty.'

'Is all labours of the pen lofty?'
inquired Mrs Brackenburn. 'The circular
of the Netherlaw warehouseman, who is
clearing off his entire stock at an immense
sacrifice, quoting prices fabulously low, and
offering bargains so rare and recherché as
to astonish all ladies and all gentlemen who
see them : is that lofty?'

'That is not literature.'

'No? Yet the writers of such circulars
must be clever in their way. Who are
they, I wonder? Needy journalists, authors
of rejected pantomimes, or what?'

Dugald could not tell. Such a field of
inquiry was far beneath his scope. He was
not one to speculate how the other half of
the world lived.

On cousin Jack's return, the quartette
who did not consider labour of the pen too

lofty to be travestied, were supplied with pencils and paper.

'Well, Katie,' said Mrs Brackenburn, all being ready, 'can you suggest any sweetly pretty title for our supposed novel?'

But no; whatever Miss Langbiggin might be, she was not suggestive. Cousin Jack proposed 'Three Blind Mice' as a sweetly pretty title; at the same time Mr Berwick made a point of interrogation on his paper, and submitted it to the arbitress.

'But what might be the interpretation thereof?' she asked.

'Anything you choose. Indefiniteness might be in its favour. But call it "Which?" if you like; "Which?" by the author of "How Much?"'

'That is the name—thank you, Mr Berwick—"Which?" by the author of "How Much?" And mind, good people, that you exaggerate sufficiently.'

'How is this game played? What are we to do?' said Miss Langbiggin, looking helplessly up at Mr Berwick, who was mending his pencil. He smiled at her, and replied,—

'You are to fancy that "Which?" is a novel—foolish or clever, as you please— and that you are a critic, at whose nod poor authors tremble.'

This, however, was a stretch of fancy impossible to the young lady; and when the papers came to be collected, while the others had produced two criticisms apiece, Miss Langbiggin was discovered to have stuck fast in her first sentence, thus,—

'I think that it is a very nice book, and I think it is very—'

The second adjective had been a stumbling-block too formidable for her.

'Never mind, Katie,' said Mrs Brackenburn; 'we make all the pleasanter women, I daresay, for not making good critics. Now, Jack, be our clerk, please. Read to us the opinions of the press.'

Jack accordingly unrolled one of the papers, and began,—

"In this we have a work well calculated

to shake the soul.   The phosphorescent "—
oh, I say, Marionette, what's this ?   Hallucinations ? phosphorescent hallucinations ? '

' Scintillations,' corrected his cousin.

' I wish you wouldn't indulge in hierogly-
phics, then.   Your penmanship is like nothing
in the world but a cuneiform inscription.
Look here ' (lifting the paper upon which
was indited in sharp even characters, with
smart tails to the ys and elegant loops to
the long letters, Miss Langbiggin's opinion
of the niceness of the book), ' this is what I
call a good lady's hand.'

Mrs Brackenburn took the reproach meekly.
The reader proceeded, ' " The phosphorescent scintillations of genius leap out every-
where—a master spirit speaks from every
page.   This book does not belong either to the
milk-and-water or to the blood-and-thunder
class of fiction.   It is unique.   We get below
the surface here, and feel ourselves put *en
rapport* with universal nature—now, here is
the intense subjectivity of the writer—"
What do you mean by such tall talk, Mari-

onette ? What is "intense subjectivity of a writer"?'

'Try and find out for yourself, Jack; the effort will impress the result on your memory as my governess used to say when questions were inconvenient. But you tax our patience as badly as a preacher who comments on every verse of a long chapter, before sermon.'

Thus rebuked, Jack once more went on :—

' "Nowhere is the intense subjectivity of the writer more subtly illustrated than in the duel scene. As we read, we hear the beating hearts of the antagonists, the plashing of the brooklet, and the cawing of the rooks. Nothing, we confidently assert, more powerfully natural has been given to the world since the Homeric age. The characters are worthy of their setting. But our space permits only mention of the heroine. She enchants us. She is a creation, yet not a creation. This statement may seem paradoxical. We recommend our readers, however, to secure the book at once, and see for themselves whether the heroine of ' Which ?' be not a true creation by the author of ' How Much ?' and yet at the same time a skilful blending of the Laureate's young lady with the skipping-rope, who warns her admirer to stand aside lest she should hit him in the eye, and that charmingly artless Ruth Pinch, who playfully taps her brother's head with a rolling pin, and with such bewitching airiness compounds a steak pudding, not knowing all the while whether it may not turn out a pudding, a stew, a soup, or something of that sort. Unfortunately, we have no space for extracts ; we can only repeat, let our readers lose no time in judging for themselves." — *Monthly Magnifying-Glass.*'

' " If Plato had sent a thing like this to his publishers, or if the Stagyrite—" '

' It's my turn now,' interposed Mrs Brackenburn ; ' and I beg to inform you that that won't do.'

'Was it not yourself, madam, who told us to exaggerate?'

'To exaggerate. But that goes beyond exaggeration. We want to have just a little touch of nature, don't you see?'

'Well, well, I pass over " The Classic Miscellany," and come to the next:—"We frankly admit that we are in no condition to set an exhaustive analysis of this new story by the author of 'How Much?' before a novel-reading public. In compliance with the requirements of our position, we took up the work intending to examine it, but truth forces us to confess that about the middle of the first volume we fell asleep, nor could we afterwards compel ourselves to a resumption of our task. We do not, however, say that the book is any more dull, foolish, or uncalled-for than a thousand others that we come across."—*The Effectual Extinguisher.*'

'" *Pelion on ossa! Vinegar on Nitre!* These are not to be mentioned in comparison with 'Which?' superadded to 'How Much?' Since the days of 'Gum-arabic for

the Great Unwashed,' no sin against common sense has been committed to equal this.
When shall the sorrows of the novel critic
cease?   When will crass ignorance, wedded
to outrageous presumption, tire of sowing
broadcast over the land these crops of sick-
ening folly, arrant rubbish, utter stupidity,
and blatant balderdash?" (Oh, Marionette!)
"It is not too much to say that, throughout
these six hundred pages of blundering absurdity, there is not one solitary redeeming
characteristic: the manner is an unbroken
series of insults to the Queen's English, the
matter a continued outrage on ordinary intel-
ligence.   For his (or her, which is more
probable) own sake, we trust this is the last
time we shall have occasion to notice the
author of 'Which?' and 'How Much?'"—
The Morning Vivisector.'

'"This writer improves.   There is a purpose likeness in the handling of 'Which?'
that was wanting in 'How Much?'   The
author has also gained in depth of insight
and power of expression; but he still con-

tinues to betray a leaning towards what we hope he will excuse us for calling maudlin. There are various minor blemishes also, to which we might take exception, as, for instance, Dolly the milkmaid's preference for one part of the country over another, because of the former being ' Far mair moorisher and mair romanticker' than the latter. We do not remember to have heard language in the least like this during any of our sojourns north of the Tweed. But in spite of a few surface faults, we believe we may predict that the author of 'Which?' will yet take a very fairly respectable standing among the imaginative writers of his time."—*The Monday Well-wisher.'*

' "Which?" is exactly the question we keep asking ourselves all through these truly absorbing volumes. Between the two heroines, the pensive Sophronia and the more sprightly Eulalia, we, like the lover in the romantic ballad of 'Bessie Bell and Mary Gray,' feel our fancy falter. The tender sensibility of the one and the in-

genuous gaiety of the other, are so equally
charming that, in place of awarding the
palm to either, we must divide it between
both. But in the exquisite pathos of this
tale lies its transcendent merit. Oftener
than once during the course of perusal
(bearded though we be, we are not ashamed
of the avowal) we were interrupted by the
sobs rising to our throat. We have been
informed by a lady friend that, on asking
for 'Which?' at the circulating library the
other day, she was told that the work was
not on hand, several copies having within
a few weeks been reduced to pulp by the
tears of an appreciative public. This fact
speaks for itself; and it is, so far as we are
aware, an occurrence unprecedented in the annals of literature."—*After-dinner Rhapsodist.*'

'I am trying to imagine the sensations of
that author,' laughed Mrs Brackenburn, as
her cousin laid the last paper down. 'Rather
bewildering they must be. Don't you feel
as if you would like to read "Which?" Mr
Berwick?'

'I feel as if I should like to read "Gum-arabic for the Great Unwashed," said he. 'My work brings me in contact with the unwashed, and I might get some lights, side-lights, at least, from your writer.'

'But my writer's work was a sin against common sense.'

'Well, even so. "How knowest thou," may the distress novel-wright exclaim, "that I, here where I sit, am the foolishest of exist-ing mortals ; that this my long-ear of a Ficti-tious Biography may not find one and the other into whose still longer ears it may be the means, under Providence, of instilling somewhat ?"'

'I, too, can quote encouragement for the potsherds of the earth,' said Mrs Bracken-burn. 'Everybody knows as much as the *savant*. The walls of rude minds are scrawled all over with facts, with thoughts. They shall one day bring a lantern, and read the inscriptions.'

'*You* read that for the first time this morning,' guessed cousin Jack. 'You have heard me say that the way to find out whether or not you've got hold of an idea is to repeat it to somebody, so you are making use of us poor fellows as a test.'

'A guilty conscience speaks there,' retorted Mrs Brackenburn. 'You remember how often you have put me to such base uses, when I was unable to protect myself. But I did not read that for the first time this morning. I wrote it long ago in the extract-book I kept for pickings from my readings which cheered or strengthened me. That was in days long perished, when I was working at the cultivation of my mind.'

'Pray, let us hear about it, Mrs Brackenburn,' requested Mr Berwick.

'Alas! there is nothing to relate,' she answered. 'I was no female Goethe. I could never make anything of self-culture. I tried various subjects as mental training— metaphysics, moral philosophy — but, oh! It was grand, too, the way I would attack *Whateley's Logic;* but all I remember now of Whateley is: "Light is opposed to

darkness ; feathers are light ; therefore
feathers are opposed to darkness." But
enough of me. Tell us something about
yourself, Mr Berwick. You were talking
a moment since of your work among the
unwashed ; is it true that you have become
a teetotaler to please them ?'

' By no means to please them,' said Mr
Berwick ; ' to strengthen my influence with
them rather.'

' I see. And are very rabid on the
subject ?'

' As rabid as can be.'

' Like the temperance lecturer who fore-
tells for all who even touch " the intoxi-
cating cup " a drunkard's grave ?'

He only laughed in answer to that.

She laughed too. Then her eyes assumed
a mischievous expression. She set pencil to
work again, and after a few minutes' scrib-
bling, passed a scrap of paper to Mr Berwick, saying,—

' With my best wishes for the cause.'

And Mr Berwick read,—

'EPITAPH ON A TEETOTALER.

'HIC JACET one who could not think
Of looking at fermented drink ;
But then, 'tis said, that he would eat,
Unheard-of quantities of meat.
He ate so much, he ate so fast,
Beef, mutton, poultry, could not last.
So great demand reduced supply,
Till, "Lynch the Gourmand" was the cry.
Death heard, and lynched him on the spot—
Lo ! here he lieth, *next the Sot !* '

Meantime Mr Urquhart remarked to his companion that this literary criticism they had been listening to displayed 'a vast amount of misapplied ingenuity.'

Ursula thought the people to be envied who possessed such ingenuity.

' The great thing, I believe,' returned Mr Urquhart, ' is to possess a well-balanced mind—a mind which can discriminate between wholesome relaxation and what might be called buffoonery.'

Mrs Brackenburn's ear caught the organ tones.

' Oh, life would' be too tasteless without a spice of " what might be called buffoonery " to flavour it,' she cried. 'Would you banish nonsense from the world altogether if you had your way?'

'Decidedly,' said Mr Urquhart.

'Then I am glad to think you have not any vote in the matter. Nonsense is a good thing in its own place; not as daily food, of course, but as a salad; and—'

Dr Brackenburn's entrance at that moment put a stop to his lady's vindication of buffoonery.

CHAPTER VII.

THE CONTRARIETY OF THINGS.

'The best laid plans o' mice and men
Gang aft agley.'

THE newcomer threw a pair of black gloves into his wife's lap. The lady drew them on, and her hands were lost in their depths.

'Do you know what is the meaning of these pretty things?' she asked Mr Urquhart.

'Not I,' he said; and his look added, ' neither do I care.'

'So ignorant of the usages of your country!' she exclaimed, not in the least quenched by the what-is-that-to-me manner of his reply. 'What a shame, Dugald! These signify, then, that my husband has been at a wedding, in his official capacity. Our Laighbieldites would scarcely think themselves legally married unless they gave a pair of gloves or a white silk pocket-handkerchief to the officiating clergyman. Have many such blessed your basket and store yet, Mr Berwick?'

'A few. But umbrellas, that are lost or exchanged the same week as received, are the blessings which usually fall to me,' said the minister of Auchterbrechan.

'And smoking-caps,' insinuated cousin Jack, 'and slippers; your fair parishioners pile up these upon your shrine?'

'Do they? No; that is all an idea about smoking-caps and slippers and fair parishioners. *My* fair parishioners are very shy of me.'

'But didn't the earl's daughter give you a penwiper?' lisped Miss Langbiggin.

'She did; the merry-thought of a fowl got

up like an ecclesiastic, in gown and bands.
My aunt thinks it a great hit as a likeness,
but I decline to see that.'

'Your aunt must be right,' said Mrs
Brackenburn. ' I never knew her wrong
yet. Your aunt is the nicest woman in
Laighbield (myself not excepted !), and the
handsomest. Miss Berwick much reminds
me of your Aunt Marjorie, Dugald.'

The idea ! Mr Berwick's aunt, an un-
lettered countrywoman, likened to Dugald's
stately Aunt Marjorie.

'Can't say, I'm sure,' was the frigid
rejoinder ; 'not happening to have the
honour of Miss Berwick's acquaintance.'

'Yes,' pursued Mrs Brackenburn, ' Miss
Berwick is one of those large-natured, sympathetic women, who make creatures such as
I understand a little how it must feel to have
a mother. She is tall and large and handsome, like Mrs Cassillis, too—*so* handsome.
On Sundays sometimes I just give myself
up to the pleasure of looking at her. I have
a special dispensation from my husband, you

must know ; he lets me off from paying particular attention to his sermons in church,
seeing that I listen meekly to so many
sermons at home.'

' My wife would hardly need to have a
rigidly literal interpreter,' observed Dr
Brackenburn, looking down at her indul-
gently.

Cousin Jack shrugged his shoulders. Mr
Berwick smiled. Mr Urquhart said to himself, ' How utterly preposterous is all this
babble ! '

Dugald and his cousin Matilda could not
shine in the same firmament : in Mrs Brackenburn's vicinity a man of sterling qualities
had no chance of doing himself justice ;
near Mrs Brackenburn everything but false
flash and meretricious glitter was ignored.
Strange it was that Dr Brackenburn, marvel
of erudition as he was said to be, should
permit, nay, even countenance, such con-
temptible prattle.

But Dr Brackenburn wanted ' a rest, a
change ; ' that was all. And this his wife

supplied ; yes, and for him, far more effec-
tively than would have been done by any
Ursula Elvester or Katie Langbiggin in
the world.   So the little woman talked
nonsense, and the others encouraged her ;
and Dugald sat disapproving and apart,
till a messenger came in hot haste for Dr
Brackenburn.   A Laighbield slater had been
killed by falling from the roof of a house in
the neighbouring village of Dykeside ; and
none but the minister must break the news
to the man's family.

Mrs Brackenburn followed her husband
downstairs, her laughter hushed, and big
tears gathering in her eyes.

'Oh, I am sorry,' she said.   'I saw George
Choppin on Saturday coming from the public-
house ; and oh, Alan, I laughed (was it not
wicked ?)—laughed at what ought to have
made me sad ; and now I shall never, never
be able to do anything for him to make
amends.'

'Never for him, Matilda ; but there are
many such left.'

'Could I go with you to see if I might be of use?'

'My dear, it would not do,' and Dr Brackenburn unclasped the slim fingers which clung about his arm. 'You forget your friends; besides, you are better away from a scene so painful as that will be where I am going.'

'Why better away? Am I so tender that I must not even go near another woman in her suffering, in case my feelings should be too much harrowed? Is not this selfishness?'

'There is no selfishness in staying away from scenes of distress, when your witnessing them would do no good to anybody. And I know from experience that you would do no good there to-night. To-morrow you shall see what service can be rendered.' With that he kissed her and went away.

Wonderfully quiet and subdued she looked when she returned to the drawing-room. Dugald, who so strongly objected to his cousin's liveliness, must be pleased now, one

would imagine. But not at all. The sobered
face, the lashes scarcely dry,—what of these ?
Tush ! Affectation, sham sentiment, the
assumption of an attitude intended to be
interesting,—nothing less or more. It was
too much to ask one to believe that Matilda
Brackenburn could really feel for the family
of some slater or other who had accidentally
got killed. This criticism of his hostess,
however, came in merely by the way ; for
he had once more established himself a
fixture, by Ursula, to whom he talked on
unceasingly, his subject :—I, my, mine, me.
He wound about, and in and out, telling of
the wonders he had looked at, the pageants
he had taken part in, and the words of
wisdom he had spoken, to his own supreme
satisfaction. We each have our weakness.
Even Mr Urquhart had his. And Mr Urquhart's was a propensity to confuse himself with his cousin Glen, and, so confused,
to appropriate lavishly of the experiences
and conversation of Captain Cassillis.

Ursula knew nothing about this mistaken

identity illusion; she only did know that,
if ever a woman was weary of a man's talk,
she was that weary woman now. At an
early hour the little party broke up, and then,
for the first time since their formal hand-
shaking, Ursula came in contact with Donald Berwick. Being sooner ready than Miss
Langbiggin, she went into the hall, and there
found the minister of Auchterbrechan waiting for his lady. He was studying the baro-
meter; but turned at her approach, ready
either to speak or to be silent, as suited her.
It was hers to decide. Well; what was
past and gone between them had left no
traces upon him, and certainly it was not
her place to remind him, by anything in her
manner, of what he had so wisely forgotten.
So she must speak.

'I suppose Auchterbrechan is quite an important little sea-port?' she remarked.

This was the extreme of common-place,
sure enough. She knew that, but could not
help herself.

'Important as Cornrigshire goes,' he said;

'but I am afraid that Auchterbrechan is not an interesting place to talk about.'

'Not so interesting as Laighbield?' she asked.

'Why, no,' he answered; 'in Auchterbrechan we haven't got any factories.'

This was ironical. He did not choose to be patronised and made to talk about what his questioner did not care for one jot, but only mentioned in order to give something to say to him. Then fearing that he had been rude, he put irony aside, and inquired if Ursula had been through any of the Laighbield bonnet factories. Ah, those factories! Mr Berwick's thoughts naturally turned to one of them, of course.

'I have not been,' said Ursula; 'but my sister Jenny has. She likes to see into such things; she is so very practical.'

'Is Miss Elvester quite well, and your other sisters?'

'Thanks; yes. They are all well. My sister Christian is not with us now, but is a governess in Netherlaw.'

She coloured a little when she said this; it was a very sore point with her.

'I was in Netherlaw the other day, and saw your sister driving in the park,' said Mr Berwick. 'She did not observe me, however.'

'If she had, I am sure she would have got the carriage stopped, that she might speak with you. She is—we are all—so glad to see anybody connected with Shetland.'

For Ursula had now come to the conclusion that she might as well speak freely of her lost home, since to refrain only made her think about it all the more.

'It seems such a long, long time since we left,' she added, with a sigh which would not be repressed. 'Do you often have tidings of Bresta, Mr Berwick?' (The pretty way she had of saying Berwick!)

'I hear once in a while from Gledcairny,' was the answer. 'I believe I shall be wanted there early in summer to marry him. I did not expect, when leaving Bresta, to be quite so soon back again.'

Ursula involuntarily drew a step closer to him—he could not even suspect her of patronising now,—and there was a strange longing in the grave, blue eyes that gleamed through their long jet fringes. Mr Berwick was going back to Bresta. Then, to be beside him made one almost feel as if one were a little nearer home. *Home!* Poor Ursula.

'But whom does your friend marry?' she inquired.

'Don't you know? I suppose you must have heard. He marries Miss Ulla Gier.'

But Ursula had never heard till now, and she exclaimed,—

'Ulla Gier to marry the doctor of Bresta!'

'Oh, but it is all right,' said Mr Berwick; 'he is of a family as good as her own, even though he is only the doctor of Bresta.' He spoke in the most matter-of-fact tone, not letting the sneer, if sneer there was, touch the sound of his words at all.

'I was not thinking of that,' she returned, with a gentleness which surprised him. 'My wonder was about not having been told the news by anybody at home, in Shetland, I mean.'

No more could be said, for just then Miss Langbiggin appeared, and her Mr Berwick had forthwith to attend on her way.

Mrs Brackenburn was thoroughly dissatisfied with the turn matters had taken. What business had cousin Jack to usurp Mr Berwick's place with the one lady; and it was even more provoking that Dugald Urquhart should so completely have monopolised the other. But having now seen Miss Langbiggin safely off in charge of the proper man, she tried to right the remaining wrong also, by inciting her cousin Jack to escort Ursula. But Jack said,—

'What! drive a friend mad with jealousy? No, I thank you, Marionette.'

'Come, be a good boy,' she insisted. 'You are not much to brag of, I daresay; still, I should like you to find favour in the eyes of Princess Ursula.'

'There must be no fighting,' said Jack. 'I am a man of peace.'

'Who thinks of fighting? And just confess, now, isn't my princess every bit as
charming as I told you?'

'Every bit as charming as you told me,'
echoed Jack.

'If I were a man, would *I* stand by and
see somebody else win such a girl, when my
chances were at least as good as his?'

But Jack was obdurate.

'She is too costly for every day,' he said;
'and I am like Beatrice in my tastes. I
would not have such a mate, unless I could
have another for working-days.'

So his cousin was left to bewail the con-
trariety of things, and to ponder upon the
futility of all human schemes; and Mr
Urquhart was Ursula's present portion.

Dugald had always some sanitary hobby
to ride. Just at present it was that all pul-
monary complaints might be mainly traced
to incaution, and would be little heard of if
persons would but adhere to one very simple
rule: on going out at night the lips must be
kept tightly closed, so that the air, instead of

being taken into the lungs at once, should
reach them by way of the nostrils; this for
ten minutes, after which the mouth might
safely be opened, and the air permitted to
descend in its raw state to the now prepared
lungs.   When she heard this theory pro-
pounded, Ursula took courage.   She would
walk home so fast that little time for conversation would remain, and she did.   Dugald,
in dumb show, entreated her to take more
leisure; but either she was blind or would
not see, till at last he could hold out no
longer, and, leaving his lungs at the mercy
of chance, proceeded to remonstrate.   'Why
such speed?   Was it not pleasant to linger
under heaven's crystal canopy, watching the
silent march of these glittering stars?'   But
pleasant it assuredly was not, with Mr
Urquhart as a companion, and less pleasant
than ever, when Mr Urquhart had ceased
to imitate the *silent* march of the glittering
stars.   Not every night is one thrown into
the company of a poet; but this foolish girl
did not appreciate the privilege.   So far

from that, she entered The Brae thinking, as she drew her breath with a sense of liberty and relief, that while Mr Urquhart might be an excellent man and an estimable member of society, anything like the oppressiveness of his manner she had never before endured.

But she had soon something else to occupy her.   An open letter lay on the table.

'From Hilyascord,' said Miss Elvester. ' Ulla Gier is to be married to that young doctor at Bresta.   It has come as a surprise on all the connection.   What—*what*, in the name of common sense, is the meaning of this ? '

Her exclamation was caused by the sight of an apparition gliding through the half-open door.

' I wanted to tell Ursula,' explained the ghostly visitant—for it was only Ulrica in her night-dress, — 'and of course she has been later than usual to-night.'

' You unconscionable little soul, you ought to have been asleep two hours ago ! ' cried Miss Elvester.

' I took Christian's telegram with me, on

purpose that I might keep awake,' avowed
Ulrica.

Ursula was startled.

' Christian's telegram ? ' she repeated.

' Here it is,' said Ulrica ; 'a messenger
from Braidmoss brought it. Isn't it mysterious ! '

And she handed the slip of brown paper
to Ulrica, who thereupon wonderingly
read,—

' " From Christian Elvester, Netherlaw, to
Miss Elvester, The Brae, Laighbield.

' " Can't stay here longer. Shall be with
you to-morrow. Early train." '

CHAPTER VIII.

A HEROINE IN SPITE OF HERSELF.

> ' There's a lake in the midst,
> And round its banks tall wood that branches o'er,
> And makes a kind of fairy forest grow
> Down in the water.'

IT was while Mr Urquhart was flying from before the face of one young lady that he found himself thus suddenly at the feet (or at least in the state of mind which was equivalent with him to being at the feet) of another. Miss Kirkpatrick was on a visit to Craigie Urquhart. No doubt Moncrieff called this Maryanne Kirkpatrick a ' bore of a girl,' resented her inconvenient propensity for hunting after patterns and stitches, and commented most

disparagingly on her personal appearance.
But with people of Moncrieff's stamp friend-
ship does not in the least debar from criticism,
and it is more than likely that Maryanne had
on her side many a flaw to point to in the
character of her dearest Moncrieff.

It is seemly that a young lady should be
engaging. But Miss Kirkpatrick was too
engaging. Her friend's brother, at all events,
considered her so ; and when she playfully
reprimanded him for having absented himself
altogether from the bazaar, and called him
'You naughty, naughty man, you!' he felt
that it would not do ; so piously remembered
various relatives whom he had not visited for
some time past, and, under cover of previous
engagements, got himself securely away.

Miss Kirkpatrick had been more affable
to Mr Urquhart than he could bear, yet hers
was not that impartial sunshine which freely
blesses all. Her sunshine was discrimina-
tive ; none of it was wasted upon—governesses for example. To Christian, who with
her charge partook of Moncrieff's hospitality

one day about this time, Miss Kirkpatrick's
manner was not only not affable, it was
even a little less than civil, and at Craigie
Urquhart Christian was for the first time
made to feel how uncomfortable the position
of a governess may possibly be. Moncrieff
did not herself take any active part against
Christian, but if Maryanne chose to do so
what cared she? For was it not quite true,
as Maryanne said, that Miss Elvester was
made over much of by Aunt Marjorie—
treated, indeed, far more like a daughter of
the house than a dependent; and did not
Glen, too, always hold her up as a pattern
to one? That was the really aggravating
bit. If Maryanne, then, liked to snub Miss
Elvester a little, no harm was done, and
Miss Elvester was only served right.

Christian, who had come to Craigie
Urquhart not to please herself, but because
Mrs Cassillis wished her and Willie to spend
a bright spring day in the country, fared
pretty much as the unbidden guest of the
proverb is said to fare. And besides having

to ' sit unserved ' she had to sit alone,
while, under one pretext or another, Willie
was kept apart from her and petted out-
rageously by Miss Kirkpatrick, whose love
for children was a phase of character de-
veloped for the occasion. So, forsaken,
Christian found her way to the great gallery
that ran along the top of the house, and
tried to make time go faster by wandering
up and down, studying the allegorical frescoes
which covered the vaulted roof, and reading
the French legends attached. Here she was
presently joined by Willie, who had made
his escape from Miss Kirkpatrick's caresses.
After a thoughtful promenade of the gallery by her side, he asked,—

' Miss Elvester, are *you* a lady ? '

Christian hoped and believed she was.

' I was *sure* you weren't just a woman ! '
he cried.

' My dear Willie, all ladies are women.'

' Yes ; but aren't some only women and
not ladies ? And Miss Maryanne says you
are—'

'Hush, dear; don't tell me.   It isn't right.

'But why isn't it right?'

Christian had not time to say why, for just as the question was asked, Miss Kirkpatrick came tripping in search of the questioner.

'You bad, little rogue!' she exclaimed, snatching the truant up.   'Why did you run away, when I was so good to you?'

'I was tired; I wanted my Miss Elvester,' he replied, with the candour of extreme youth.

'But you'll come with me now, darling. Cousin Moncrieff and I are going out, and you'll have such great fun.   Come, Willie.'

'I beg your pardon, Miss Kirkpatrick,' interposed Christian; 'but he will only be in your way.   I am quite sure he had better stay with me.'

Such harshness!   Miss Kirkpatrick was astounded.

'How *can* you grudge the poor thing a little pleasure?' she ejaculated.   'Tell your governess, ducky, that she must let you come. Cousin Moncrieff will show you such lovely, beautiful things.'

'What sort?' inquired Willie, with some curiosity.

'Just come and see,' said Maryanne.

'I want to go and see,' cried the child.

'Miss Urquhart asked me to fetch him,' added Miss Kirkpatrick, 'and she is mistress in *this* house; isn't she, Miss Elvester?'

Christian's face flushed. She understood the situation perfectly, and how it was intended to bring a contest about, but Christian would not condescend to fight. She quietly yielded the point, therefore, and suffered Willie to be taken. Immediately afterwards she too went out to the grounds, for she dared not lose sight of her charge. She must be at hand to receive him back when his present companions should wish to get rid of him.

Christian had never been to Craigie Urquhart before, and as she crossed the park outwards, she turned to have a good look at the place, so as to assure herself that her eyes had not been playing her false when she arrived in the morning; that the mansion-house was really like what it had then appeared to her. This second view fully confirmed the impression left by the first. Such a mingling of odd whimsies and freaks had surely never before been perpetrated in the name of architecture. What school the original building might belong to, no man living could tell. It had been improved upon, and overlaid, and heightened, and widened, and broadened, until now you could not so well say that it had been added to, as that it *was* additions.

Passing from the park, Christian came next into the shrubberies. Mr Urquhart's shrubs were cut into patterns, Dutch style ; and they were his special pride. No shrubberies in Scotland touched his, he was fond of telling people ; and if by 'touching,' he meant coming near in strange fantasticality, he may well have had reason for the boast. Yet, in spite of their owner's glory in them, one could not help fancying that the plants must feel and resent having been clipped so out of all similitude to nature.

Out of the shrubberies into the woods,
where the moss was spangled with prim-
roses, and the trees were awake and waiting to be dressed. Having emerged, Christian climbed a knoll, from whose height
could be descried, looming through its smoky
vapours, miles away, the tallest chimney stalk
in Netherlaw. But she never even glanced
at that ugly reminder; her whole attention
was given to a picture in the hollow on her
other hand.

A lake just large enough to sail a pleasure
boat on; happy Willie throwing pebbles into
it; Moncrieff and Maryanne sauntering arm-
in-arm through the trees that fringed its
margin. The air was full of soft brightness; over the ground lay a suggestion of
green—the shadow of coming summer cast
before; the voices of the birds went in
pleasant unison with the audible pulsing of
the water.

Christian was just taking notice how high
the bank was, and how, instead of sloping
gradually towards the lake, it stood steeply

up all round, when—a plash! a succession of
shrieks. The child was struggling among
the rushes. Miss Kirkpatrick seemed petri-
fied past both speech and action ; those calls
for help came from Moncrieff.

'A rope! get a rope!' cried Christian, as
she made her swift way by ; and then she
flung off her heavy outer garments, and
plunged into the lake. To swim came as
easy to the Shetland girl as to dance ; so she
was fearless—fearless for herself, but in terror
indescribable about the child. Happily she
did not lose her presence of mind. Watching
her opportunity, she caught the unconscious
boy as he rose to the surface for the last
time, and so kept afloat till help came. Fortunately the gardener's house stood near, and
Moncrieff's cries being heard there, the child
and his governess were soon safe on dry
land.

Willie required a good deal of care and
nursing for some time after this ; but
Christian took no harm from her wetting.
The affair got into the local papers

though, and was made the very most of there, so that Mrs Cassillis's governess became, to her own extreme confusion, a sort of nine-days' wonder in Netherlaw—a heroine in spite of herself.

CHAPTER IX.

WHY CHRISTIAN COULD NOT STAY LONGER
IN NETHERLAW.

' We'll draw thee from the mire
  Of this (save reverence) love, wherein thou stick'st
  Up to the ears.'

'LET one be really good and noble
through a lifetime, and likelier
than not it is never heard of,'
Christian was driven to exclaim impatiently
these days ; ' but just do something a little
out of the way, and though it may not have
cost you an effort, what an ado everybody
will make about it.'

Miss Urquhart's view of the case was
somewhat similar. She wondered why there

should be such a bother. Christian was
lauded to the skies for having saved the
child, and Moncrieff was quite passed by;
whereas, in effect, Moncrieff had saved both
the child and Christian; for if she had not
screamed so loudly, nobody would have
known of the accident and come to the
rescue. Yet not a soul thought of saying a
single word about her in the matter. One-
idead that she was, however, Moncrieff before long had the vexation in question replaced in her mind by anticipations of the
forthcoming Bachelors' Ball.

Now, about the date of this most select of
Netherlaw gaieties, Craigie Urquhart became
uninhabitable for the time being. The whole
house was thrown into confusion, in order
that the gas-pipes, laid only a few years
before, might be lifted again, Dugald having
somewhat fallen upon the alarming discovery
that gaslight is unfavourable to longevity.
Turned out of Craigie Urquhart, Moncrieff
lost no time in effecting a comfortable settlement for herself at Argyll Gardens. Mrs

Cassillis had gone from home to pay some visits, taking Willie with her for his health's sake, and only the governess remained. It was barely a week since Christian's trip to Craigie Urquhart, but Christian did not allow the remembrance of that day to affect in the smallest measure her treatment of Moncrieff. So she listened patiently to many hopes and doubts and fears before the ball, then lent a helping hand to adorn the beauty for the ball, and subsequently gave ear to a full and particular record of the belle's so brilliant course throughout the ball. After all which, she was very ready for a change of theme—any theme, she said to herself; even Aunt Euphemia's church politics would come as a relief.

Moncrieff at last got tired of the topic herself, and as there was none other to supersede it, gave voice to the wish that one could get rid of the dulness and stupidity of things in general by going to sleep for a week or a fortnight at a time. She was dawdling between the front and back drawing-rooms when she said this—a picture of utter aimlessness.

Christian, busy at her usual forenoon fancy-work among the flowers, was arranging prim-roses in a basket of moss. It was pleasant to watch her about it, she being one of those women with that soft, caressing manner of handling things, which imparts to the on-looker a peculiarly restful sensation.

Glancing up at her listless companion laughingly, she said,—

'To sleep for half the year might be better still; never to have had an existence, would not that have been best of all?'

It would require an impossibly great men-tal effort to lay hold upon the idea of never having existed at all; but to sleep during one half of the year, that Moncrieff could grasp, and that she did not approve of; for what, in such a case, of ball toilets, skating cos-tumes, spring bonnets on the one hand, of the summer and autumn equivalents of these on the other? Oh no, indeed! even though you did find yourself reduced to the extremity of boredom now and then, as things were, you would not be so absurd as to wish for a sleep half-a-year long. That ridiculous notion disposed of, Moncrieff had a demand to make.

'Do put some of those Glen lilies in my hair,' she said, stopping before the crystal bowl, where a number of the flowers in question floated amidst their supple, long green leaves.

She was instantly gratified. Two of the yellow lilies were taken out of the water and set against the intense darkness of her hair. There not being a mirror, great or small, in either of the drawing-rooms (that was a whim of Glen's), the beauty, for want of better, declared that she would look at herself in Miss Elvester's eyes. This was freely permitted, but with a result which scarcely pleased Moncrieff: one's neighbour's eyes are by no means flattering looking-glasses, she found. The sight of herself there sent her off at once to seek reassurance at proper quarters, an expedition from which she presently returned completely satisfied.

'Do you know,' said she, coming and placing her arms round Christian's shoulders —not from affection, but she wanted something soft to lean upon, 'I almost begin to wish I hadn't had my front hair cut. Glen doesn't like it.'

'What a pity,' sympathised Christian. 'And how obliging of your cousin to advise you about your hair-dressing.'

'But isn't it really ill-natured not to admire the fringe? I do wish he wouldn't be so odd. Fancy his calling earrings a remnant of barbarism, just as if the more civilised you were, you didn't have the handsomer earrings. Is it to please Glen that you have laid them off, Miss Elvester?'

Christian put up her hands, and pushed away the hair from a pair of the smallest, prettiest ears.

'I never wore them,' was her reply. 'My eldest sister cannot bear the fashion, and none of us have had our ears pierced.'

Christian's eldest sister's opinion and Christian's family's ears were subjects which did not tempt Moncrieff to glance at them even aslant. She quitted her support, and wandered to the window to reconnoitre; for a conveyance of some description had stopped at the door.

'Here is Aunt Euphemia,' she announced discontentedly. 'She is lecturing the cab-driver, and her jacket is like a sack, and her bonnet as bulging as a tea-cosy. She will want me to go into town with her—I know she will. But I can't go; I caught a dreadful cold at the ball; you know I did, Miss Elvester.'

'You forget to tell me,' said Christian; 'for indeed I've not heard of it till now.'

'Oh, I feel quite ill!—yes, I do!' cried Moncrieff; and she hurried to the dining-room, wrapped herself in a sofa-blanket, dropped into an easy-chair, simulated a cough to the best of her ability, seized the morning's *Reflector*, and fixed her eyes steadily upon the leading article;—such was the fear she had of being carried by Mrs Cassillis of Baronshaugh to any of the ecclesiastical councils which that zealous Free Church-woman was in the habit of frequenting. What the newspaper had to do with the performance is not so clear. Probably Moncrieff felt that anybody seeing her reading an editorial must directly be convinced that she was very much out of her usual indeed.

Christian, meanwhile, went on with her work. Five or ten minutes passed, and she was in the act of carrying a flower vase from one stand to another, when Moncrieff came back, with scarlet cheeks and in a state of high excitement.

'What is wrong? what is wrong?' cried Christian, thoroughly frightened.

'Oh, but it is too dreadful!' pouted Moncrieff. 'Cousin Glen has been killed—too, too dreadful!'

Christian's hands fell by her sides, the vase lay in fragments about her feet. She gazed at the other girl with horror-filled eyes, and her face was as drained of colour as Moncrieff's was flooded with it.

'It is all in the papers,' went on Moncrieff.
'I saw it by chance just now. Another
officer shot him by mistake, and he is dead.
It has given me such a shock;' and she
flung herself full length on the lounge, crying
that it was too cruel, and then got up again,
declaring that she was going to be ill—she
was sure she was going to be ill.

At this crisis entered Mrs Cassillis of
Baronshaugh, solemn and severe. After
brief scrutiny of the white-faced figure that
never moved from among the fragments of
the vase to give her greeting, she throned
herself upon the piano-stool—because it was
the only seat with no back to it.

'Good morning, Miss Elvester,' said she.
'It is a pity you have broken that orna-
ment. Mrs Cassillis valued it on various
accounts. She will never be able to get it
replaced.'

Oh, how the harsh tones jarred! Christian tried to say that she was sorry for the
mischance, but words would not come. She
stooped, and with trembling hands began

mechanically to gather together the scattered pieces.

Aunt Euphemia now turned her attention to Moncrieff.

'You have raised a most foolish, a most needless ado,' she said. 'If you had taken time to read the paragraph to the end, you would have seen that it refers to another man altogether—a retired naval officer in the south of France.'

The grating tones sounded quite melodious now. But the sudden relief following upon the as sudden alarm made Christian giddy, and she had to take hold of the nearest piece of furniture for support.

Moncrieff, not at all impressed by the homily which Aunt Euphemia went on to deliver on the duty of making sure of a matter before proclaiming it, started up, threw away her grief like a garment, and gave lively vent to her satisfaction. She would have felt really sorry, had Glen been dead, but since he was not dead, she de-

voutly thanked Heaven that mourning would
not be required, for—

'Nothing in the world is so unbecoming
to me.'

'I will tell you what is a great deal more
unbecoming to you,' said Aunt Euphemia
grimly, 'that cropped hair overhanging your
brow. Yes, my dear; that is unbecoming
in every sense of the word. What would
Saint Paul have said to such a fashion, do
you suppose?'

'Oh, he was an old bachelor, of course,'
rejoined Moncrieff disrespectfully.

She, too, was of opinion that 'They didn't
know everything down in Judee.'

'The apostle of the Gentiles was a
widower, it is now believed,' corrected Aunt
Euphemia.

'Was he, indeed?' responded careless
Moncrieff. 'How funny!'

'Not in the smallest degree funny, my
dear. But to keep to the subject: I ask
you how any well-reared young woman can
feel that it is proper to go about the world

reminding all who look upon her of a convict ?'

'Good heavens! Aunt Euphemia!'

'Moncrieff, I beg and pray that you will give up the use of such an unlady-like, not to say unchristian expression.   And I repeat it with perfect deliberation,—your hair is cut on the convict's pattern exactly.   Something, it appears to me, must be radically wrong with the moral sense of any one who voluntarily assumes the fashion of a felon.'

Felon had an even more offensive sound than convict.   But who would be cast down by criticism coming from the wearer of such a jacket ?—of such a bonnet ?—assuredly not Moncrieff.

Christian had meantime recovered her self-possession ; and to her the lady of Baronshaugh now returned.   Mrs Cassillis would fain know the cause of this agitation.   What was Captain Glen to Miss Christian Elvester, that the young lady should break a costly vase to shivers when told that the young man was dead ?   Sud-

den deaths among one's acquaintances happened often, and yet one was not over much
perturbed.

An idea dawned upon Moncrieff.

'Oh, it is too absurd!' she said; 'but
you must be in love with cousin Glen; are
you, Miss Elvester?'

A look was Christian's only answer.

'It is true, it is true!' chanted Moncrieff
provokingly; 'you may not deny that it is;
you would if you could, but you can't.'

'A statement of that sort needs no denial,'
said Christian with dignity.

'But it's true! but it's true!' insisted Moncrieff, in her aggravating sing-song. 'Dugald
said so before, only I had forgotten. Did
not Dugald say, Aunt Euphemia, that Miss
Elvester was quite plainly setting her cap
at cousin Glen? and didn't Aunt Marjorie
tell him that—'

'Such vulgar language, Moncrieff, is most
abhorrent to me,' interrupted Aunt Euphemia;
'and it is, in the circumstances, highly inde-
corous besides. If Miss Christian Elvester

has, unfortunately for herself, been guilty of any imprudence, it is no subject for flippant jesting.   It is a grief to me that you are not more seriously disposed.   If, instead of balls and theatres, you would accompany me—'

'Excuse me a minute, I believe I've left my handkerchief downstairs,' said Moncrieff; but no sooner was she outside the door than she looked in again, and catching Christian's eye, waved the said handkerchief towards Aunt Euphemia, whose back was turned, and indulged in a little pantomime of triumph at her own cleverness, ere she finally withdrew.

Christian paid no attention to Moncrieff.

'What have I done, Mrs Cassillis ? What imprudence have I been guilty of ?' she inquired.

'Your position here has been one of peculiar difficulty and delicacy,' returned Mrs Cassillis of Baronshaugh, nothing loth to explain. 'I have said from the first that you are too young and too — ahem — too attractive for the post. Your employer, however, believed that she knew best; and she looked on you as a young lady above any sort of manœuvring.'

'And I am above manœuvring,' said Christian. 'And I don't think anybody will accuse me of having forgotten on what footing I came here; though Mrs Cassillis would have made me forget it if she could.'

'There can be no question about that, Miss Christian Elvester; and Captain Cassillis (who has been frequently at home since his regiment removed to Mucklestanes, *too* frequently, I think) has also, I daresay, done his best to make you forget.'

Christian would not answer this; how she felt may be imagined.

'My nephew's freedom of manner towards young ladies is distinctly reprehensible,' proceeded the Lady of Baronshaugh; 'I do not judge *you*. You yourself know what object you had in coming here, and with what object you remain.'

'Do you mean that I—' commenced

Christian, but got no further; she could not put anything so repugnant into words.

'I say nothing about *you*,' returned Mrs Cassillis; 'nothing, except that you will not be consulting your own dignity if you remain here longer; and that you had better go home to your sensible sister and let her take care of you: that is my opinion, Miss Christian Elvester, and my advice.'

'I thank you,' said Christian in a low, but quite steady voice; 'I will go home. After what you have said, nothing would tempt me to stay. As for Captain Cassillis, there has been nothing in his manner towards me such as you imagine—nothing; not a shadow of blame rests on him so far as I am concerned.'

'His attentions to you, I repeat, have been distinctly reprehensible!' cried Mrs Cassillis of Baronshaugh.

'Captain Cassillis has paid me only the attention which any one in his place would naturally pay to any one in mine; but excuse me, please, from saying or hearing more on such a subject;' and, with a manner quite wonderfully like that of Princess Ursula, Christian passed from the presence.

So Mrs Cassillis of Baronshaugh had at last relieved her conscience by taking sure measures for getting rid of what she had all along held to be a serious mistake in the household of her sister-in-law; but not thinking that the riddance would be an immediately accomplished fact, she turned to other matters for the time. Christian, however, had no idea of delay. Not an hour must be put off. She would not, could not, should not wait for the return of the mistress of the house. She rushed at once into the thick of her preparations.

Presently, to the door of the chamber came Moncrieff. It was locked; but locks did not instruct Miss Urquhart. That Christian chose to deny herself was nothing, if Moncrieff chose not to be denied.

'Do, *do* let me in,' the besieger cried. 'What is the sense of being disagreeable and cross?'

What was the sense indeed? And yet, though one did almost exempt this butterfly from the onus of moral responsibility, one could not but feel a little resentful after *such* things had been said.

'Don't be silly; there's a good creature,' persisted Moncrieff. 'I have such a piece of news for you—something quite too comical. Won't you open to me?'

So Christian was obliged to open to her.

'It is a great secret, of course,' said Moncrieff, as she came triumphantly in. 'Aunt Euphemia is to be married in a week.'

Christian had, ere now, on hearing of some unlikely match, taken a resolution to be surprised at no matrimonial announcement evermore. But such vows are seldom kept.

'Your Aunt Euphemia to be married!' she echoed in a sort of amused horror—'to be married!'

'To Dr Doig Sledgehammer,' said Moncrieff. 'I think Dr Doig Sledgehammer must be rather mad, you know. Aunt

Euphemia calls him an apostolic man ; but
I don't believe the apostles ever wore such
boots—so creaking, and as big as boats.
Cousin Quentin will have a new parent now
—how droll! But he will marry as soon as
he comes of age, of course. Should you like
to be Lady of Baronshaugh, Miss Elvester ?'

'Not I,' said Christian.

'I should,' frankly avowed Moncrieff. 'I
am going there to-morrow,' she added, 'to
stay till after the marriage with Dugald and
cousin Quentin. Aunt Euphemia has an
appointment with Dr Doig Sledgehammer
now ; I wouldn't keep an appointment with
such a bugbear, I know.'

'Dr Doig Sledgehammer, like Saint Paul,
is a widower,' supposed Christian. Moncrieff
nodded an affirmative.

'And the Sledgehammers,' she said, with
lowered voice and air of mystery, as if this
were a dark subject, and only to be handled
with gloved words, 'are all blue-stockings ;
they read Hebrew and study laws of things ;
they will never be married.'

'And that is everything, of course,' said Christian, putting up her lips.

'Governesses have generally to be old maids, haven't they?' presumed Moncrieff gaily.

'They haven't a quite fair chance, perhaps,' suggested Christian; but satire, however well aimed, had a way of glancing harmlessly aside from Moncrieff. She smiled divinely therefore (at least any of her numerous admirers would have said it was divinely), and opined that even governesses might sometimes marry 'Old Calabar missionaries, prison chaplains, or persons of that sort.' Then the notion seized her to indite a note to Glen, congratulating him on not being the Captain Cassillis who was lately shot, and off she went, never having asked the meaning of, or in any way remarked upon the confusion in the room. Her utter want of interest was certainly convenient sometimes.

Until this day Christian had not herself known how deep was her interest in Glen Cassillis, and even now she would fain have persuaded herself that she was not that much-scorned creature, a woman who has given her heart unsought, that she cared for the man only in a friendly fashion, as for one who had been very kind to her always. Much could be said of the feelings which afflicted the girl this unhappy afternoon—pages might be filled, but silence is best. There are feelings which one seems to have no right to meddle with.

Delivered from Moncrieff, Christian completed her arrangements, and wrote to Mrs Cassillis. Mrs Cassillis of Baronshaugh, she stated, had spoken in a way which made it impossible to the writer to remain at Argyll Gardens. She begged to be forgiven for her breach of engagement; she returned thanks for the great and unvarying kindness which she had ever received; and she would always remain Mrs Cassillis' obliged and affectionate Christian Elvester.

And now to send a telegram to The Brae, that the edge of her sisters' astonishment might be off before the cause of it should appear. On her way she came face to face with Miss Kirkpatrick, and was passed by, without a sign of recognition. The incident provoked a smile, and the reflection,—'What great people we Elvesters used to imagine ourselves, and now we are too low in life to be acknowledged on the street by the young ladies of Netherlaw.'

Threading the public thoroughfares has a certain effect in diverting the mind from private vexations; so making her way through busy Netherlaw, Christian lost distinct consciousness of her trouble. It remained, of course—as the dull pain of headache remains, though you may not every moment be thinking of it,—but she had that feeling which one experiences when mingling with a crowd, that curious sensation of merging personality in the great throbbing life of the multitude.

In the spring sunshine Netherlaw was looking its best. Royal Square had even an air of freshness about it: indeed, the crocuses growing in the centre part were as like country crocuses as possible. Passengers were bustling about the station; tarriers for a night were gazing from hotel windows; street arabs with merry whoops were forming a procession after the jail van, and making miraculous escapes every minute from the cabs, spring carts, and lorries which passed and re-passed in uninterrupted stream; infant newsvendors were spreading newly-printed bills of evening-paper fare upon the pavement, wherever room could be found. One of these catalogues lying across Christian's path, she informed herself that it began with 'A lively scene in the Town Council,' and finished with 'Dr Doig Sledgehammer on the Union Question.'

A year since the girl might not have known what this Union Question was; now, thanks to Mrs Cassillis of Baronshaugh, she was well aware of the civil strife being waged in the Free Church camp, and of how these Christians loved one another; and of the certainty of a second Disruption, should the proposed union with a sister dissenting body be carried into effect.

This very afternoon Mrs Cassillis of Barons-haugh and the Rev. Dr Doig Sledgehammer, violent anti-unionists both, had been at a meeting of those like minded with them-selves, taking private counsel together how they might put a check upon the troublers of their Zion, and when Christian looked up from the news-bill, it was to behold this august pair turning a corner within a few feet of her.

'He has fallen away to the Voluntaries,' the lady was saying, and she pronounced 'Voluntaries' with more virus than if it had been 'Incendiaries.' 'As for the other, he stands openly convicted of heresy—most pestilent heresy. Dr Sledgehammer, I say, if such as he be not made example of, the ancient glory of Scotland has departed from her.'

'True, true, undoubtedly. Ay, un-doubtedly,' rejoined the able divine, her companion,—whom, by the way, I do not mean to describe; one dares not rashly comment upon the person of an apostolic man.

'The Westminster Confession set at
naught, the Standards disregarded, veiled in-
fidelity taught in more than one of our pulpits,'
resumed the lady of Baronshaugh ; but here
her eyes fell on the governess from Argyll
Gardens, so she stopped both discourse and
motion, and while her friend went slowly on,
waited to have speech with Christian.

Christian in Royal Square was no business
of hers, but there are persons who arrogate
to themselves the right of looking after everything and everybody ; who would like nothing
better than to

> 'See that the angels keep tune,
>   And watch that the sun and the moon
>   Do not squander the light they have got.'

She tapped the wanderer's shoulder, therefore,
and required the reason of a young lady
being abroad by herself at an hour when the
counting-houses and offices were sending
forth their hundreds.   An errand to the
General Post-office, was the explanation.

'Was your letter one which could not

be entrusted to a servant?' Mrs Cassillis would like to know.

And Christian saw that she was suspected of a secret correspondence on the spot.

'My letter was of no consequence,' she said; 'I came on purpose to send a telegram to my sister.'

'Money must be rife with you, Miss Christian Elvester, if you can afford to correspond by telegraph. I myself rarely use anything but post-cards now—a great annual saving, I can assure you. But young people have no idea of economy.'

Economy being a favourite theme, she might have descanted long enough on it, but for the fact that Dr Doig Sledgehammer awaited her under the shadow of St Barnabas, in consideration of which circumstance she contented herself with a few general ideas.

Sometime later, driving westward, she espied among the pedestrians thronging Lockerbie Street Christian Elvester again, and—ah, yes, to be sure!—that vain-glorious coxcomb, Fyfe Armstrong, the artist. It was to be seen now why our artful little governess should make errands to Royal Street at this unseemly hour. Glen Cassillis not to be had, a would-be genius would serve, at least for flirting purposes, instead.

But had communication of a telephonic nature been possible between Mrs Cassillis and the pair she suspected, the flirtation would have been found to be of a very harmless character indeed. Christian was disparaging Netherlaw, as strangers always will; Mr Fyfe Armstrong upholding it, as natives always do.

'You talk of our mists,' said he; 'is there *no* mist in Shetland?'

'Yes,' she admitted, smiling—'dreamy, silvery haze. But, pardon me, what Netherlaw calls mist is coffee-coloured, suffocating fog, which one wants to cut one's way through with a knife.'

'Well, I give in about the fogs; but fogs, notwithstanding, there are good points about Netherlaw. This very street, for instance— this long, wide, broad-pavemented Lockerbie

Street : look at the gay shops here, the handsome houses with lawns and shrubberies
about them yonder, and say if we have
not before us as fine a promenade as anybody could desire.'

' The unfortunate thing about me is that I
don't appreciate promenades at all ; but that
may be because I haven't the poet's gift of
seeing the inner meaning of things.'

' Ah, Miss Elvester, you are sarcastic
now.'

' Not I,—only common-place. Don't you
keep telling us, you artists, that what we
every-day people see is but the outer husk of
what we look at ; what you seek for is the
truth within. I should like to get beyond
the symbol, if I might ; will you not help
me ?'

' How, pray ?'

' Poets as they can, as it is revealed to
them, interpret Nature's picture-language for
us. Be an interpreter, then. Streets are
not Nature's works : of what are they the
picture-language, please ?'

And thus—and thus—went the ' flirtation'
on.

At the Western Cross these two young
persons parted.   The one, as she went up
Argyll Gardens, said to herself,—

'What spirits Mr Fyfe Armstrong is
always in.   I shouldn't think anything ever
ruffles him.   How happy he!'

The reflection of the other at the very
same time was,—

' That pretty creature is just a trifle too
sunny for a sombre world ; and you never
can be quite sure that she isn't laughing at
you ;—" dreamy, silvery haze, indeed!"' and
his lip curled Byronically as he ran up the
steps of a rather imposing house in a rather
imposing terrace, and admitted himself with
a latch-key.

Mist was a sore point with him to-day.
Upon his easel had lately been a coast-
scene, appointed to fill a vacant space on
the dining-room wall in the town residence
of Mr Baillie Geddes.   The special charm
of the painting lay, as the artist himself

believed, in the half-revealing, half-conceal-
ing veil of mist flung lightly over the faces
of the neighbouring hills.   Not so judged
the Netherlaw art patron : the picture had
been returned to the studio in a hurry, that
it might have ' all that confounded fog
rubbed off.'

So Mr Fyfe Armstrong's heart was hot
within him, and his spirit as chafed as
Christian's.   Yet meeting by the way, these
two had completely deceived each other,—
this happy young man, and that creature so
sunny as to be somewhat out of keeping
with a sombre world.

Early next morning, while Moncrieff was
still balmily slumbering, Christian set out for
Laighbield.

CHAPTER X.

APRIL FOOLS.

'Och-hon ! for somebody,
Och-hey ! for somebody.'

IS not *if* the weightiest syllable in the language ? In every affair of life we find it. *Yes* and *no* are qualified by it ; hopes and expectations, fears and anxieties, hang upon it ; regret, remorse, repentance, take up and echo it ; and sometimes its consequence is greatest when seeming least.

Now comes my fateful *if*.

If Moncrieff had penned the congratulatory note to Glen at the time intended, her cousin would have smiled over the billet, and there would have been an end. As luck would have it, however, something or other came between her and her purpose, and two days passed before she actually sat down to write.

She was at Baronshaugh ; and, oh, but time was travelling at a snail's pace ! Not rosy hours nor laughing hours ; but long, dark, dreary hours were for the present appointed her. The once delayed letter would never have been written else. Shut up with Aunt Euphemia, even letter writing, so troublesome at other times, became a resource.

It was the first of April. Spring showers were plenteously watering the earth ; far too plenteously, thought Moncrieff, for in such weather she could neither visit nor expect visitors. And this was what gave its peculiar intensity to the dulness from which she suffered. Her brother shared the confinement ; but he, being a poet, was not so greatly to be pitied. He could compose odes to rain drops, or visions of cloudland, and so solace himself.

While Moncrieff wrote, Dugald occupied

the music-room, striking chords in a forcible manner, and giving utterance to baritone cadenzas of various lengths and degrees of intricacy. His was the order of voice which, inacceptable in solo singing, serves passably well as background for a chorus ; but we do not hear ourselves as others hear us, and Mr Urquhart's own private belief was, that if he should choose to become a singer by profession, more than one public favourite might bid the stage farewell.

While Moncrieff wrote and Dugald sang, Quentin was out in the rain, for the first-named had made a 'gowk' of her easily-imposed-on cousin, by despatching him to the manse on the false information that Mrs Brackenburn had sent, urgently desiring to confer with him.

And while Moncrieff wrote and Dugald sang and Quentin was out in the rain, Aunt Euphemia sat opposite her niece in the library, reading, with knit brow, " The Ten Lost Tribes : An Enquiry and an Inference. By Susannah Inverarity."

This work had been sent to Baronshaugh, 'with the author's compliments,' for which reason Mrs Cassillis—unlike another friend of ours in Laighbield, who skimmed recklessly the books presented with authors' compliments, and afterwards, if pressed sore for an opinion, broke into admiration of type and binding—would conscientiously read it to the last sentence, and would not fail subsequently to inform Susannah Inverarity that she, the author of " The Ten Lost Tribes," did diverge in various essentials from sound doctrine as set forth in the Standards and the Westminster Confession.

Moncrieff having done with Glen, thought she might next devote a few minutes to Maryanne Kirkpatrick, from whom she had received several sheets of effusiveness in the morning, and by whom she had been lovingly besought to ' write by return.' So she would, just for once in her life, write by return. Perhaps you might like to see a specimen of Miss Urquhart's epistolary style. Look here, then, and admire.

'MY DEAR CREATURY,—I wish it would
stop raining. Everything is so *stupid* when
it rains. Aunt Euphemia is to be married on
Tuesday in a hotel at Netherlaw, but that is
a *secret*, so I mustn't tell. Nobody will be
there. She says there is *no occasion for mum-
mery.* They go to *Jerusalem* for the honeymoon, and we stay here with cousin Quentin
till the workmen are out of Craigie Urquhart.
Do come and see us ; won't you ? I wish
Miss Elvester would call (she's not *really*
Miss Elvester, you know, but one can't call
a governess Miss Christian) ; but she never
comes near me, though she *must* know how
very dull I am. But it's because she's so *mad*
with me for finding out that she is so *awfully
in love* with somebody. He was thought to
have been killed, and she *nearly fainted.* She
couldn't *then* deny being in love, so Aunt
Euphemia gave her *such* a scolding, and said
she ought to leave Argyll Gardens *at once ;*
and early next morning she left. It's too
funny to think of her being so fond of somebody, when, *of course*, somebody never *looks*

at *her.* Poor somebody doesn't know that
I am engaged to cousin Quentin ; it isn't
exactly an engagement, but *we understand
each other.* I've been writing to somebody
just to *please* him ; he thinks so much of a
letter from me. If you come, bring me some
nice books, delightfully wicked, like "A
Fiery Furnace." Dear somebody was so ab-
surdly shocked when he saw that at Aunt
Marjorie's. I had to say it was Miss Elvester's, and that made her so vexed. Of course
you know *somebody* means *cousin Glen.'*

When she had written so far Moncrieff's
hand felt cramped, and her head probably
was in sympathy with it ; so she got up and
wandered to the music-room, to make an
April fool of her brother, by telling him that
Maryanne was coming along the avenue.
While she was enjoying Dugald's excited
stampede to the window, her cousin, newly back
from *his* fool's errand, went into the library.

On perceiving how his mother was engaged,
Quentin, like the good son he was, refrained
from disturbing her, and quietly seated him-

self at the table which Moncrieff had quitted
a minute or so before. Taking note of the
two letters, the one unfinished, the other in
an envelope as yet unclosed, an idea stole
into his mind—his own experience suggested
it; he would—happy thought !—he would pay
back Moncrieff; he would make an April fool
of her, as she had made an April fool of him ;
he would change these letters. He had barely
carried into execution his daring design, put
the unfinished letter into the envelope, and
spread out the letter which had been taken
from the envelope in the other's place, when
Moncrieff re-entered.

Gloomily she came, for Dugald, instead of
appreciating her pleasantry, had been very
disagreeable ; had even gone the length of
saying that if she would imitate the graceful
dignity of demeanour which characterised—
Miss Ursula Elvester for example—it would
be an untold improvement on her present
style. But she brightened considerably on
seeing Quentin, and took great credit to herself for having so adroitly befooled him.

'Oh, but I say, Mrs Brackenburn thought it wasn't much fun,' remarked the subject of the joke. 'She said she wouldn't play tricks at all, unless she could invent more clever ones than that.'

'Plain-faced people are always so fault-finding,' rejoined Moncrieff. 'Don't you think so, Quentin?'

'Oh yes, of course,' acquiesced the accommodating young man. 'But look here, you know,' he added seriously; 'unless you're quick about it your letter will be too late. Sandy always takes our mail-bag an hour before the time.'

'How silly of him,' said Moncrieff.

'But it isn't him,' replied Quentin, oblivious of the requirement of the verb 'to be;' 'it is mamma; she is such a one for being in time.'

'Well, Glen's can go; this other doesn't matter,' decided Moncrieff. And she sealed the envelope and handed it to Quentin, who took it to Sandy, who bore it in the mail-bag to Laighbield.

Quentin not coming back, Moncrieff, after trying in various ways to murder time, and finding that time would not be murdered, once more approached the writing-table, that she might look over what she had said to Maryanne. But, lo! what had she here? *This* sheet commenced with ' Dear cousin Glen!' How could such a thing be? She appealed to Aunt Euphemia; but Mrs Cassillis was unable to throw any light on the phenomenon.

' Your letters have remained precisely as you left them,' was her reply; for she, pursuing that heresy-hunt through the pages of Susannah Inverarity, knew nothing about Quentin's feat of legerdemain.

' You must have folded up the wrong letter,' said she, as her niece continued to exclaim. ' Very careless, indeed. This will be a lesson to you.'

Whenever anything untoward happened to one, Aunt Euphemia's sure consolation was that ' it would be a lesson.'

Moncrieff protested that she had no need

of the lesson, had not been careless, had never folded any wrong letter up. The letter was still unfinished; how, then, *could* she have folded it up?

'There is only one alternative,' said the elder lady. 'Do you imagine that it folded itself?'

'Perhaps it did; or if it didn't, it might have been the spirits,' opined Moncrieff.

'The spirits! What spirits?'

'Those we called last night, and waited for so tiresomely. They couldn't come then, but they must have come to-day; and *they* have changed my letters (it was at this table we tried table-turning). I know I've heard of changelings before; and—'

'Table-turning, Moncrieff! Do I hear you say that such a sinful delusion as that has been practised under this roof?'

'It was Matilda Brackenburn and her cousin Jack, Aunt Euphemia; *I* didn't care for it one bit. Indeed, cousin Matilda made us do some very silly things. We had to sit wishing, all of us at once, that Quentin, who had been sent out of the room, would do whatever we fixed on. But when he was blindfolded and brought in, he didn't do anything; he only stood. Cousin Matilda said we couldn't have been wishing hard enough; and I know I hadn't, because I had forgotten what it was we were wishing for, and so wished instead that we mightn't have any more of those stupid games.'

Very righteously indignant was Aunt Euphemia on hearing this. Mrs Brackenburn was compared to Elymas the sorceress; the playing at Spiritualism denounced as 'hidden works of darkness,' and great was the ado. But Moncrieff's letter concerned her more than all the judgments predicted as coming upon spirit-rappers. She must recover it; and she must be her own messenger, for servants were such bunglers. So she left Dugald to bear the brunt of Aunt Euphemia's rhetoric, carefully encased her beauty in waterproof, and sallied through the wet.

It was what farmers call 'a growing day,'

and the buds and tender herbs could almost be seen to sprout; but Moncrieff looked neither at tree nor grass—neither at children playing in the puddles, navigating the most delightful canals, formed by deep cart-ruts, and filled with rain—nor yet at any illustration of life or character whatsoever, till she stood in the presence of the postmaster of Laighbield.

Mr Mungo Mauchline was in meditative mood. He, even he, had been made an April fool of by some light-minded jester of the town : he had paced from end to end of Cassillis Street with a paper between his shoulders, announcing in large letters,— 'The top flat of this clay tenement to let.' So when Moncrieff appeared, the martyr was pensively musing on the petty trials which intellectual superiority to one's compatriots brings. The treatment of Dante by an undiscerning Florence would, if Mr Mungo Mauchline had ever heard of it, have seemed an entirely similar case to his own treatment by Laighbield.

But here was a lady from Baronshaugh,
so putting aside consideration of his griev-
ance for the present, he tip-toed forward
with his courtliest grace of action to receive
Miss Urquhart's commands.   Moncrieff had
never for a moment doubted that her mission
would be successful, and she believed Mr
Mungo Mauchline to be mildly maundering
when, in answer to her demand, he said,—

'Happy as I would be to obleege one of
your honoured family, ma'am, this is the
single straw on the camel's back, so to say,
wheech I am not fit to handle.   Us officials
being underneath Government shupervision,
our rules is strong and stric' ; a letter once
posted by the public is posted for ever.'

'I sent the *wrong* letter,' represented
Moncrieff ; 'it was a *mistake,* so of course
you must *give it back.'*

She thought that a sprinkling of emphasis
would have the desired effect.   But no !

'I could not do it,' said Mr Mungo
Mauchline, slowly nodding, and patting the
counter with two of his fingers ; 'nut though

every avoidable argument was projooced; nut even though the Queen, or Mrs Dr Brackenburn herself, was to implement the requist.'

This, then, was serious; and Moncrieff became so much the more importunate. She must have the letter; she *must* have it. She would give the postmaster five shillings— half-a-sovereign — a guinea — anything he liked to name, if only he would place that letter in her hands again.

The sight of beauty in distress is a moving one, no doubt; still, an official under Government supervision must be of iron nerve and inflexible will; moreover, the offer of a bribe was highly offensive to Mr Mungo Mauchline.

'Never did I expec', ma'am, to be obleeged to refuse a favour to your beauteous sect,' he cried, with pathetic dignity; 'but if anny party in the public poseetion held by me was once to breck through our by-laws, it would certainly introjooce havoc into the very core of the postal system. As the Earl of Corn-

rig said to me, when he stepped in here not
long ago, to soleecit my vot for his friend,
the gentleman wheech is now the honour-
able M.P. for this county,—says his lord-
ship, in his free and friendly way, " I know
you, Mr Mungo Mauchline, for an honest
man." '

A customer who had entered in the course
of this reminiscence, flung herself into conversation in the easy fashion prevalent at
Laighbield.

' My troth, Mungo,' she exclaimed, laughing, ' but ye *ha'e* some airy anes !'

'Wheech lets you perceive, ma'am,' proceeded Mr Mungo Mauchline, treating the
interpolation with the silent contempt befit-
ting it, ' that to any practice savouring of
corruption, I am, and always will be, deaf
and blind.'

At last Moncrieff became convinced that
there was no hope for her, and thinking
herself the most hardly used person on
the face of the globe, she returned to
Baronshaugh to inform her cousin that

Mr Mungo Mauchline ought to be immediately deposed, and a postmaster less rude, stupid, and disagreeable appointed in place of him.

But, as it soon appeared, the laird himself was an even greater offender than the postmaster. Quentin met Moncrieff in the hall, and rallied her on her wild-goose chase, and with much giggling informed her,—

'*You* are the gowk now, you know; mamma didn't see me at it, but *I* changed your letters.'

Two days afterwards, Moncrieff's letter was returned to her under cover, with the words :—

'Miss Urquhart must be more careful in future how she manages her correspondence.

'G. C.'

She immediately replied :—

'DEAR GLEN,—It was *mean* to read a letter

that came to you by *mistake.*   I will never
forgive you.   MONCRIEFF.'

   '*P.S.—I* don't want it *now.*   You can
keep it.'

What reproach Moncrieff conceived to lie
in sending the letter back, is beyond being
guessed at.
   To this arrived the answer on the morning
of the 6th,—

   'DEAR MONCRIEFF,—It was only when I
had read as far as your letter went, that
I saw it could not have been meant for me.
I shall make a shift to struggle through existence unforgiven.   GLEN.'

And there the correspondence ceased.

CHAPTER XI.

PROPOSING.

Independence, o'er the day preside :
Propitious power ! my patron and my pride.

MISS ELVESTER was of opinion that Christian's abrupt departure from Argyll Gardens was decidedly out of order. An engagement was an engagement; the governess of one Mrs Cassillis had nothing to do with what another Mrs Cassillis thought about her, provided the governess's own conscience were clear. And even if the strong provocation did make it justifiable to forsake one's post, it would have been a braver thing to stand by the post until all one's duty had been done. It

was over and past, however, and this poor
Christian need not be made more unhappy
than she was by any course of lecturing, nor
should. She had come home; and home
ought always to be a refuge from trouble;
what she had to do for the present, therefore,
was simply to rest, and to make believe to
herself that there was no such thing in the
world as ' Independence.'

And Christian did what she could to follow
this advice, but the rest that fell to her was
curiously like restlessness, and the make-
believe was no belief at all. As the days
passed, too, her restlessness increased; for
she had expected some message from Mrs
Cassillis, but no message came. Could it be
that Mrs Cassillis, merciful Mrs Cassillis,
considered her unpardonable? Surely so,
else there would have been a reply, if not to
Christian's own apology, at least to the letter
which Miss Elvester had written since. With
this, then, as well as a private matter which
no soul must ever discover, fretting her, it
may easily be understood that her state of

mind was not a very enviable one just now.

The 5th of April dawned and darkened, and on the 6th Miss Elvester, sitting among her girls, read aloud the announcement of Dr Doig Sledgehammer's marriage to Euphemia Rhynd, widow of the late Laird of Baronshaugh. During the comments which followed, a caller, Dugald Urquhart, was shown into the drawing-room. For the first time in their acquaintance Christian felt glad to see him. Surely now she must hear something about the household she had taken French leave of the other day. In this hope she was disappointed. Dugald only said,—

'So you are tired of Netherlaw, Miss Christian. I don't wonder at your, at any one's, preference for the country; there is a freedom, a genuineness about it that is most invigorating.' And then he enlarged on the aspects of rural scenery, which pleased him most, and discoursed of 'blues,' and 'greys,' and 'pearl-tints,' and 'sheens,' and 'shimmers,' and 'effects,' and 'glades,' and 'azure distances,' and 'vague shadowy vistas stretching into space.'

Into the first opportunity which presented itself, Miss Elvester edged mention of the marriage which all Laighbield was discussing to-day.

'Yes, it took place at Netherlaw,' said Dugald ; 'a strictly private affair, most strictly private.'

Not a word more by way of information did he vouchsafe ; it never was his custom to expatiate on any sayings or doings save his own—and such of other people's as he appropriated. Christian saw that what she would know she must ask ; therefore, watching her chance, she inquired if Mrs Cassillis and Willie Ruthven were home yet.

'Home! No—that is—well, in fact, I'm not certain whether they have returned or not,' said Dugald. 'My sister could, I daresay, give you all the gossip,' he continued, 'but *I* never bear such things in memory. Indeed, I had almost forgotten the reason of my present visit : you left a piece of your

property in my sister's possession, Miss
Christian; she found this clasp, or buckle,
or whatever its designation is, among her
belongings after you were gone.'

Saying which, he produced a small brooch
of Roman mosaic which had been lent by
Christian to Moncrieff some week or two
before, and handed it back to its owner. He
spoke of it as a clasp or buckle, because not
to know the name of a feminine trinket gives
a certain air of superiority to a man, and is
rather calculated to produce an effect upon
weaker minds; and he said that it was to
return this clasp or buckle that he had come
to The Brae, because one is not always
obliged to display his real motives. The
true cause of Dugald's call divulged itself
in the manner of a postscript: his cousin,
her sister, and himself were going to ride
this afternoon; his sister would be delighted
if any of the young ladies here would join
the party. His cousin's people could mount
two—Miss Ursula was said to be a famous
horsewoman; would she care to go?

Ursula looked at Miss Elvester, meaning her, if she saw any objection, to say so.

'My sister will be seriously disappointed, if you cannot join us,' declared Dugald, smiling towards Ursula insinuatingly.

Ursula might possibly believe this; she knew no better. But the thought of Moncrieff's disappointment was nearly too much for Christian's gravity. Meantime, Miss Elvester said neither good nor bad; but the eager face of Ulrica caught Ursula's attention, and decided the matter. Ulrica had over and over again cried lately that she would give anything—almost the hope of authorship itself—just for a good canter over the country. And now that the pleasure was within reach, it would be cruel to disappoint her of it. Accordingly, the invitation was accepted (Moncrieff's invitation), and Dugald went out well pleased, and nothing doubting but that his footing with Ursula was perfectly secure. Of this fond notion the sisters did not dream; not even Christian, who knew him best, had any idea that Mr Urquhart's ambition soared so high as to lead him to imagine that he might have Princess Ursula for the asking.'

Ulrica's joy was boundless.

'You meant not to go,' she cried, hugging Ursula with a fervour more flattering than comfortable; 'but you looked at me, and you changed. It was so beautiful of you. And Mr Urquhart is as unlike his cousin Quentin as possible. He is quite a wise, intelligent person; is he not, Jenny?'

'Vastly so, evidently.'

'And handsome too. Only there is something about him that makes you think of the gentlemen engraved on the bills which used to come to Chapel Street, you remember, that you might choose what kind of coat you wanted, if you were a man. It is unfortunate a little; but still, Mr Urquhart is much finer looking than *your* Captain Cassillis, Christian.'

At this unexpected termination the colour flew to Christian's face, which, being conscious of, she coloured all the more.

'*My* Captain Cassillis!' she said. 'Not mine, indeed ; it is very unlikely that I shall ever see him again.'

The indifferent tone in which the words were given was highly satisfactory.

'I should think you'll be sorry for that,'. rejoined Ulrica ; 'for you elevate him high over everybody else's heads. I know you do.'

'You foolish Ulrica.'

'Yes,' persisted Ulrica, 'I am half a witch. I often, oh, ever so often, when I look in people's faces, know what they are thinking of. I have great in—in—in*tuition.*'

'People's faces don't think of anything,' quietly corrected Ursula ; 'and I'm afraid you talk too much about yourself, dear.'

While Christian's conclusion was, that one must be very clever indeed, so to guard a secret that her own people shall not suspect her of having any secret to guard.

A little while, and Ursula with Ulrica set out for Baronshaugh. Shortly after, Christian returned to the drawing-room, and found her eldest sister leaning back in a lounging-chair, doing nothing. Nobody could lay want of energy to the charge of Miss Elvester; yet she was not one of those rather uncomfortable women of whom their friends proudly tell you, 'Never will you see her idle'—whose fingers must every moment of the day be occupied; hers rested now and then, just for a change. She said that she could always think out anything more thoroughly when her hands were still. And she was thinking now. Her ruminations had been on the same subject as Christian's; for when that young person leant over her sister's shoulders, saying,—

'I'm sadly out of patience, do you know. When are we to come to the question of what is next to be done with me?'

It was replied,—

'I have been turning over that very question now. You are most anxious for its settlement, I suppose?'

'Sure enough, I am anxious.'

'Yes. And one sees that your longing is still for independence; so be it. But are

you ready just at once to lay yourself open
to "kind requists" for "pearsonal interviews,"
and all the other delightful experiences
which fall to the lot of a governess out of
a situation?'

'Jenny, dear, I want, before searching for
any other situation, to fit myself for one. I
can only play at being a governess as it is;
but I should despise myself were I to go on
so. I can't be an idler. I more than ever
want to do real work, if I only knew how.'

'You are ambitious; but you feel that to
do real work, preparation is necessary.'

'You told me once to be content with my
day of small things; and so I tried to be,
and was. But it would not serve for always.
I don't like the thought of never getting
from the foot of my profession; it does not
matter just now, but when I come to be an
elderly woman, I shall want to have some
position.'

'Well?'

'Jenny, you *have* the most disconcerting
way of saying "Well," as if you expected to

be told what was really worth hearing, and
would be surprised and shocked at anything
common-place.'

'Be as common-place as you like, my dear,
I shall neither be surprised nor shocked.
Tell me, will you, how you found out your
deficiencies?'

'I had no high opinion of myself to begin
with; but I used to meet people who made
me feel what a cypher I was, by asking about
my theory of teaching, and what particular
method I followed. And then I saw governesses who had universal history and biography at command, as well as—as—oh,
well, as the royal genealogies of Oviedo;
the internal laws of the Burmese Empire;
by how many miles Mount Chimborazo out-
runs Teneriffe, and all such lore. Think of
that, and then of me.'

'I do. Naturally, you were found wanting,
when balanced against so much learning.'

'I saw that as I was, I should never do.
I must have a theory; but where to find one,
Jenny? And I must have a multitude of

new facts, as well as a much firmer grasp of old ones.'

'You must, in short, study hard for a year or two, fitting yourself for the sphere you seek to enter. I knew it from the first, my sister; what I did not know, and greatly doubted was, whether your wish to work would wear. That was best proved by just letting you make trial of your strength. Contact with the reality of the thing would send the fancy flying soon enough; but it has been more than idle fancy, as it seems.'

'I think it has; at any rate it is stronger than ever now. I did not speak when I was with you in winter; but I had already made up my mind that I was only losing time at Argyll Gardens, and that, as soon as my year was out, I must give up the pleasant, easy life I was leading, and ask you to let me come home to study. I may stay and study now; mayn't I, Jenny?'

'You may certainly study, but not at home, I think. Home study is apt to be a desultory affair. You shall go, rather, to the

Hanoverian School, where Ursula and you were boarders formerly. There you can grasp well your facts, and make choice of your theory. That place, at least, seems to me the likeliest. Does it please you ?'

'Of all things it would be best; but, Jenny, the expense!'

'Is my concern. You will infinitely oblige me by confining yourself to your own province.'

'I suppose I can do nothing else; but, some day, I hope I may be able to pay back part—I never can the whole—of what I owe you.'

'How dare you take that debtor and creditor tone with me? Are you not ashamed of yourself? Is it not my right to arrange such matters for you ?'

So Christian was silenced. She would never be allowed even to guess how many things Miss Elvester would have to deny herself, in order to send one of her girls to Hanover. A consideration of details followed. Then the elder sister said,—

'Well, you may consider that vexed question answered. Rejoice, therefore, in the prospect of a career. I heartily wish you all manner of success.'

'But I shall want a pair of spectacles to give dignity to me,' rejoined Christian. 'I have nothing impressive in myself; I'm ridiculously out of keeping with the idea of a career.'

'You are, rather; no, you're not exactly what we call a capable woman—not one who would have been quite after the heart of King Lemuel's mother for a daughter-in-law. Yet, for all that, you may have the teaching faculty within you. I hope so, sincerely, since without my sweet girl graduate, neither spectacles nor anything else will very much avail.'

'I won't have the spectacles after all, I think. I want to be learned, not to proclaim myself so; for I did not so greatly like the ladies I've mentioned, that I should care to copy them. They were too aggressive with their information; they seemed pleased only when they had put every other woman to silence; and they would talk about high art, and the Platonic philosophy, till we ignorant ones were so tired of both. And I don't believe men enjoyed it either; they like better to be the talkers themselves. I used to think that if I should ever succeed in being as cultured as they (how they did harp on that word "culture"), I would try to wear my wisdom less ostentatiously.'

'Right, my dear. Put on blue stockings if you will; only remember Sidney Smith— see that your skirt is always long enough to cover them. In the meantime, this being settled, do you suppose you can be at rest here for a few weeks?'

Christian thought of one circumstance which just at present made it impossible for her to be at rest, and after a minute, she said,—

'Mrs Cassillis has taken no notice of me. I am afraid she must have somehow misunderstood. Might I write again, or would it be better not?'

'What would you say?'

'I can hardly tell; there is so much I should wish to say.'

'Say it, then ; but be sure that you keep
your letter till to-morrow.   Read it by morning light, when, perhaps, instead of sending
it off, you may tear it up.   I have known the
like happen.   And while you are relieving
your feelings by putting them on paper, I
must be off to attend to some business of
mine in Laighbield.'

'Charitable business, of course.   Your
hands are as full as they used to be at
Eastravoe—*dear* Eastravoe—or even fuller,
Jenny.'

'And why not ?   But, truth to say, I am
obliged to keep watch over Ursula, who
would be unquestioningly benevolent.   She
would rather be deceived three hundred and
sixty-five times a-year, she tells me, than go
about suspecting everybody.   And that is a
very pretty sentiment too.   I, however, who
am of harder grain than you romantic young
people, like to find out for certain that my
charity is not a mere encouragement of idle-
ness, though it does take a little trouble, to
be sure.'

CHAPTER XII.

DISPOSING.

'I ha'e a but and I ha'e a ben,
　　Lass, gin ye lo'e me, tell me noo ;
　A penny to keep and a penny to spen',
　　And I canna' come ilka day to woo.'

CHRISTIAN had retired upstairs to relieve her feelings by putting them on paper. Yet, notwithstanding the 'so much' that there was to write, she sat, pen in hand, for fully ten minutes, with no further result than,—'My dear Mrs Cassillis.' At the end of that time tapped Mysie: Miss Langbiggin waited in the drawing-room. It is always so: just be particularly out of the humour for making yourself agreeable, and that same hour Providence will send one of the most tedious of your acquaintances to call upon you.

It was the invariable habit of Miss Langbiggin to leave to her interlocutor, both the suggesting of topics and the handling of them. And conversation on such terms was uphill work with Christian, whose inventive faculties were not in good acting order to-day—had nearly proved themselves unequal to the composition of a letter. If one could but discover Miss Langbiggin's subject. Alas! that was out of the question. Miss Langbiggin had no subject. She was at The Brae in her capacity of collector for the Laighbield Clothing Society, yet she did not know anything whatever concerning those who were to be clad. Why had the young lady become a collector? Christian ventured to inquire. Mr Berwick had spoken of it to her; that was the reason, she replied. Ah, here was a theme of mutual interest, surely!

'Mr Berwick was certain to want you to work,' Christian said; 'I know him very well — rather, I did once, when he was minister of Bresta.'

' Indeed,' rejoined Miss Langbiggin.

' Indeed' may be pronounced so as to convey strong interest, profound indifference, or thorough scepticism ; as Miss Langbiggin pronounced the word, it implied simply nothing at all.

' Isn't it the fashion here to call Mr Berwick a heretic ? ' said Christian, driven to desperate devices.

Any Free Church woman would, judging from Mrs Cassillis—now Mrs Sledgehammer —be stirred to her depths by the sound ' heretic.'

Mistaken again ! With her usual measured smile, Miss Langbiggin responded,—

' Mr Berwick is a very pretty preacher.'

Though ' pretty' was the last term to apply to the preaching of Donald Berwick ; as well might ' lively' have been used to describe the conversation of Katie Langbiggin.

When she had sat for what she deemed the exactly proper number of minutes, the

collector for the Laighbield Clothing Society
arose, and having received the contribution
of the Misses Elvester (such an extremely
correct young lady would not, on any
account, have said, 'the Miss Elvesters'),
stepped away primly down the slope.

The door had hardly closed after Miss
Langbiggin, when another hand was upon
the knocker; a man's hand now—the hand
of Captain Glen Cassillis. And Glen asked
for Miss *Christian* Elvester; thus giving
Mysie a light, with which she immediately,
and under seal of strictest secrecy, proceeded to illuminate a friend of hers who
was delving in the garden; but inability to
conceal a matter is a weakness not *totally*
confined to the feminine half of our race,
so, through the agency of Mysie's gardener
friend, the fact (fringed and decorated with
fiction according to fancy) that 'the Captain'
was courting one of Miss Elvester's girls
became known all over the valley within
the week.

As he came up, Glen had been admiring

the idyllic aspect of the quaint, small house
looking out from the tender greenness which
spring was weaving all about it. And the
room in which he presently found himself
pleased him no less; he had never beheld
an 'interior' anywhere, he thought, so perfectly picture-like as Miss Elvester's drawing-
room. Delightfully picture-like too, was the
girl who stood there, so evidently startled
at seeing him. Nor was she so love-lorn
but that she had—not indeed bound her
hair 'with bands of rosy hue,'—but at least
disposed of a bunch of violets amongst the
coils of it; and she wore a companion bunch
as a breast-knot.

Yes; Christian was startled. She was
at the same moment surprised, dismayed,
most glad. Her eyes fell before the steady
light of Glen's, and a tell-tale colour deepened
the wild-rose bloom of her cheeks. But if
she could not control her face, she would,
at any rate, be mistress of her manner; so
she answered her visitor's frankness with
something quite ludicrously like the neat,

well regulated precision of Miss Katie Langbiggin,—Captain Cassillis had come to stay
at Baronshaugh, she supposed.

'No,' he replied, 'not to stay at all; only
to see Miss Christian Elvester.'

'Well?' she said; and, unconsciously perhaps, intoned the monosyllable exactly as
she had objected to hear her sister intone
it about an hour ago.

'Do you *think* it is well?' inquired Glen,
smiling; 'or are you wondering how you
can most civilly bid me begone?'

'Oh no. You bring me some message
from Mrs Cassillis, do you not? Is she
still at Bonnyfaulds?'

'She has been at Mucklestanes Manor for
a week; and for that reason, letters addressed
to her at Bonnyfaulds, as yours was, only
reached her yesterday — they had taken I
don't know what of a roundabout by the
way. In the interval she had written to
you once or twice, and was in a puzzle
about her letters being unanswered.'

'Those letters must be lying for me at

Argyll Gardens now,' said Christian. 'I expected no letters, so did not leave orders to have them forwarded.'

Thus the silence of Mrs Cassillis was simply and satisfactorily explained. But Christian could not as yet realise the relief she felt, being in present dread that she should next be expected to throw some light on the nature of the passage between her and Aunt Euphemia. Glen, however, knowing so much more, so very much more, than Christian imagined, took good care to put no awkward questions. Instead, he talked of this, that, and everything, in the pleasant, easy way which, in time gone, had had only too much fascination for one foolish girl at least, who used to listen to him. Of his aunt, he casually remarked,—

'Now she has given herself wholly to the Church, it is expected that those outside of her own particular pale won't be worth her further notice. I, at any rate, am here under that impression, to ask you to forget (if not forgive), and—to come back to Netherlaw.'

'He could have no conception of *what* his aunt had found fault with her for,' thought Christian, 'or he would never dream of suggesting a return to Netherlaw.'

'Her conduct, I've no doubt, has been beyond speaking about,' he continued, more seriously; 'but is my mother therefore to suffer? Will you not return to *her*? She wishes it.'

Christian silently shook her head.

'Do you mean that you will not?'

'I can't; I have other plans. I am going away.'

She tried to speak firmly, but succeeded only in being pathetic. The 'I am going away' meant to sound so spirited, was very sad in the heart of it. Glen looked at her with a queer, slightly embarrassed air of scrutiny.

'And am I to tell her that you don't choose to see her any more?' he asked.

'Would she come to see me before I

leave? I should be so very glad, — but would she really come?'

He rose and went to her side—they had been sitting at some distance apart—and he said,—

'Nothing will please her better; only, you must give her a claim.'

'She has that already.'

'A vague, general claim, perhaps; she wants one more definite.'

'I don't see how it could be made stronger.'

'I do. It is a mother's claim upon you she would have. Will you give her that?'

Christian looked quickly up, and then as quickly down.

'While I have lived with her, Mrs Cassillis has been like a mother to me,' she said.

'Yes; but she wants to be more yet to you than she has been. Such is the message she sends by me to-day; and you will let her? I beg it of you.'

'I — I — don't understand you, Captain Cassillis.'

'Well, this is frightfully abrupt, I know; but circumstances leave me no alternative. In plain English, I am here to persuade you, if I can, to give me your promise that you will come back to us, not as the child's governess, but as my wife.'

There was no possibility of misunderstanding him longer; but, sure enough, it was abrupt,—and bewildered, Christian, had no answer ready. Having thus broken the ice, her wooer went on to plead his cause, and to plead it astonishingly well to, considering that he did not throughout even once utter the magic little word, love. It was strange (though Christian herself was too confused at the time to heed it) that a man should offer marriage to a girl, and yet neither ask her if she loved him, nor fill her ears with protestations of his love for her. But how was Glen Cassillis to talk of love? He had not fallen in love,—not he! only, having read Moncrieff's letter, it seemed to him that it touched his honour, seeing he had engaged, even though undesignedly, this young lady's

affections, to make her happiness his concern.
But though he was not actually in love with
Christian, he did like her very cordially.
Also, the discovery of her secret had caused
to spring up in him a new tenderness for
her; while the thought of what she must
have endured at his aunt's hands made him
not only willing but resolved, to protect
her from any future possibility of such
attacks.

If he had ever imagined that Christian
would at once throw herself into his arms,
he was speedily undeceived. Christian drew
back from him, and looked as if she would
be only too glad, courtesy permitting, to bid
him a hasty good-day. Not being carried
out of himself as the real lover is, Glen was
conscious of an odd half-amused feeling all
the while. He was not prosecuting his suit
in the orthodox way, he knew; he ought to
be more demonstrative. Yes; but if he
were to attempt anything in that line, the
chances seemed to be that Christian would
vanish from the room, which would be a

somewhat awkward consummation of so important an interview.

'My time is limited; I must be back at Mucklestanes Barracks to-night, and have to ride to Braidmoss for the train,' he said, looking at his watch.

And then he considered what an unloverly speech it was, what an unloverly action, and wondered whether his companion thought so too.

'But you won't send me away unanswered,' he went on. 'What message shall I take to my mother, if you haven't a word for me?'

'Give Mrs Cassillis my love,' said Christian, with some hesitation.

'Your love—yes; and what now for me? I have nothing dazzling to offer a woman, I know; yet I do hope and believe that if you could trust me enough to put your happiness into my hands, you should not have to repent it.'

Still Christian held back from him. She felt that very certainly she loved him, yet somehow she could not bring herself to give the answer for which he waited. Mind having a subtle influence on mind, probably the utter absence of passion in her suitor had, unconsciously to herself, the effect of so restraining her.

'You're not afraid to trust your future to me?' he asked.

'No,' she confessed, after a pause—'it is not that.'

'What then?'

'My sister and I have to-day settled about my future, and arranged that I shall go to Germany to study.'

'To study what?'

'Whatever will make a good teacher of me, and help me to rise in my profession.'

'Your profession!' he echoed, smiling in spite of himself. 'Your profession! And what have you to do with a profession, you pretty flower?'

'To live by it, if I can,' said she, lifting her head up.

There was nothing so very amusing in the idea, she thought.

'Let women who must make their own way in the world,' he rejoined, 'but do not you. Tell me, is this "profession" my only rival ? Is there no other lover before me ?'

'I never had a lover in my life,' she answered ; 'but there is my sister, Captain Cassillis.'

'And is she very terrible ?'

'You have seen her ; you know what she is ; and I can do nothing without her consent.'

'Of course, I will ask her consent ; rather, I have asked it already. Yes ; I met her under the lime trees, and we talked for, I daresay, half-an-hour. The end of it was, that she gave me leave to win you if I could. Can I ?'

He pronounced the last two words softly, persuasively ; and yet had come near to her again as he spoke. Instead of retreating this time, she turned a very little towards him. The slight motion, involuntary as it was, signified self-renouncement. Glen held out his hands.

'Your profession will be that of a wife,'
he said ; 'for you shall not go to Germany,
you shall stay with me.' Then, a second
later, 'Escape me *now*, my sweetheart, if
you can.'

Fast in so secure a clasp, it would not
have been easy; but I do not know that
she even tried ; at all events, Captain Cassillis congratulated himself that, whatever
might be said for the beginning of the interview, the final part of it was conducted
according to recognised forms. And, after
all, though a man might not be, strictly
speaking, desperately in love, this was such
a proud and independent creature (the pride
and independence would one day assert
themselves more than Glen now recked
of!), that there was a peculiar piquancy in
taking a lover's liberties with her.

When about to go, her future husband
would have the bunch of violets which served
as Christian's breast-knot.

'Oh, not those,' she said ; 'I will gather
fresh ones. I shall not be a moment about it.'

'No, no,' he replied, with the kind of authority which women do not rebel against. ' I will have none but those sweet Christian Elvester has worn.'

So, of course, she let him take them ; and then she went away.

When Glen had received Moncrieff's misdirected letter, he made no mention of the matter, excepting in those two communications to his cousin which you have already seen. Though his mother happened to be living in the same town with him at the time, he did not acquaint her with Christian's flight. So much could not well be told, without that being added by way of explanation, which no man in the circumstances could choose to add. Christian herself should be allowed to explain, in her own way and at her own convenience. As for him, his course was resolved upon ; but no mortal should ever know by what blundering chance that course had been suggested. Accordingly, when he informed his mother that he desired to gain Christian Elvester for his wife, Mrs Cassillis,

while expressing her entire satisfaction that
it should be so, did not for a moment imagine
that the desire had only now arisen. Neither
must anybody else have reason so to imagine.
There was, indeed, one who might have her
suspicions—his cousin Moncrieff; but even
should it be so, Moncrieff would for her own
sake keep silence if she hoped, as it seemed
she did hope, to marry Quentin of Baronshaugh.

If Christian herself had only guessed!
But Christian was in blissful ignorance. Sitting still where Glen had left her, she was so
very happy as to be almost afraid at her own
happiness. She had not, until this afternoon,
dreamt that Glen's regard for her had gone
beyond the positive degree ; she had sometimes even fancied that he loved Moncrieff.
But now he had declared himself her lover—
hers ; and she need no longer blush to
remember how she cared for him.

She was roused from her reverie by her
eldest sister's return. For a few moments
after entering, Miss Elvester silently observed

the bright, flushed face before her.   She
neither frowned nor smiled.   'So radiant!'
she exclaimed at last.   'The wooing, then,
has sped successfully.'

'Are you pleased, Jenny ?' inquired Christian, under her breath.   And she drew Miss
Elvester down on the couch beside her.

'*You* are, clearly; and that is of more
importance,' was the reply.   'But what of
your career now, Miss Christian Elvester?
where has your ambition vanished ? where
your unquenchable thirst for independence ?'

'I have let them all go : I could not help
it, I could not, Jenny.   Are you very much
ashamed of me ?'

'Well, is it not just a little humiliating
to think that a girl will forego her most
cherished projects of usefulness, if a lover
should but chance to cross her path, and cry,
" I want you, pretty one " ?'

Christian protested that she would not
have dropped her projects if—if the lover
wanting her had been any other than Glen
Cassillis ; and also, that while she was

content to relinquish the idea of being a teacher, she did by no means relinquish that of being taught ; she would certainly go on to learn what she could concerning the thousands of things around her, of which as yet she knew little more than the names. Then she put her arms about her sister's neck and insisted upon being kissed and forgiven. And Miss Elvester, in spite of what had been spoken regarding the humiliation of the thing, did kiss and forgive her. But in return,—

'Pray, lighten my darkness a little,' it was said. 'I have heard a good deal about Captain Cassillis from others, but never a paragraph so much from you. Naturally, I should like to hear your love story—as far, I mean, as a sister may be told.'

But Christian's love story was not to be related at this time. Another story was on the threshold—a story not of love, but of death. Ursula and Ulrica came in with white, scared faces, and the tidings that

Quentin Cassillis had been thrown from his horse: the animal had stumbled over the edge of an unused quarry, and the young laird was now being borne dead to Baronshaugh.

CHAPTER XIII.

CHIT-CHAT.

'They called for tea and chocolate,
And fell into their usual chat,
Discoursing with important face,
On ribbons, fans, and gloves, and lace.'

IT was Fair week once more at Netherlaw, but the working-man had been unfortunate in his weather. The Fair Saturday had been foul. There had been a wild, misty drizzle ever since, till to-day, Thursday, when it rained heavily again, and seemed to mean rain.

The town was forsaken both by gentle and simple — comparatively speaking, forsaken. There were still enough of the latter class left to crowd the Netherlaw Common, an extensive public green to the east of the town, where, in defiance of the weather, shows of all sorts, merry-go-rounds, and stalls for the sale of 'fairies' were driving a brisk trade. Away west, however, the forsakenness was literal. Whole circuses, quadrants, crescents, and what not were done up in brown paper ; for upper-class Netherlaw had gone 'down the water' two months ago.

Every house in Argyll Gardens was shut, and the card in the lower bow-window of No. 11 directed postmen and any others whom it might concern to leave letters and parcels at the West End Club. There was life within No. 11, however, only it was looking forth from back and area windows. It was calumniously reported (one cannot credit it !) of some Netherlaw families of the better sort that, if they could not afford to be out of town quite so long as their neighbours, they would at the proper time display brown paper like the rest, and retire behind the scenes for a month or more. But had the mistress of this house seen it necessary to stay in town all the year round, her windows would frankly have confessed the fact. So Mrs Cassillis was not to be found here to-day — she was far enough from Netherlaw. The life referred to as in the background and area was contained in the persons of Miss Urquhart, Miss Kirkpatrick, and a servant or two.

The house was not open for the convenience of Moncrieff; but Moncrieff, in town for a little shopping, was making a convenience of the house being open. The young lady had visited various warehouses in the course of the day ; had caused many yards of silk to be unfolded, many boxes of lace to be emptied, many rolls of ribbon to be unwound; had made more than one politely-smiling salesman hate her in his soul ; had met Miss Kirkpatrick at Price & Platterfill's (the fashionable Arcade Street restaurant); and was now, together with Maryanne, partaking of a cup of tea in the back parlour, where her brother had once upon a time recited before Aunt Marjorie's too fastidious governess his 'friend's poor lines.'

Maryanne, like Moncrieff, was in Nether-law only for the day, being on her way from Paris to join her family at their marine residence on the west coast. She had been several months in France, and was really quite continentalised—so much so, that she almost spoke broken English. She was now telling with honest pride of the great personages she had met, and the gay assemblies she had graced, and the wonderful excitements she had known.

'Papa protests he spent a fortune on my *toilettes*,' said she ; 'but, figure it to yourself, at some of those receptions people *didn't seem to know who we were ;* and I did really and truly feel sometimes just as if we weren't of much consequence at all.'

Moncrieff slowly sipped her tea, and, leaning back in her chair, followed with her finely-shaped eyes the progress of a fly across the ceiling. She was not paying attention to one single word. And this sublime indifference of hers had a damping effect; for even if you are talking less to entertain your hearer than to gratify yourself you like to have some slight interest taken or feigned in your historiettes. So Maryanne by-and-by stopped, stopped abruptly at the climax of a sensational description, thus,—

'I wondered what was coming next. It was *so* exciting. And I took hold of the burning taper, and just as Eugene said, "*Helas, Mademoiselle!*" I put out my hand. And there was a horrid sound like a dying shriek, and an awful crash (the ambassador supported me, or I should have fainted with terror), and, looking round, I saw—'

Would Moncrieff have curiosity enough to ask what Maryanne saw? Moncrieff would not. After there had been silence for a moment, Moncrieff said,—

'What a bore rain is. I wish it would clear up.'

'You are a horrid, selfish thing!'—this was Maryanne's innermost thought—'and it serves you well to have lost both your cousin Glen and Baronshaugh.'

But men with pretty, unengaged sisters, and girls with handsome, highly eligible brothers, cannot easily rouse the open resentment of their friends; therefore, though Miss Kirkpatrick was not good-natured beyond the rest of her kind, she answered amiably, and said,—

'Ah, how this *triste* weather and that unfortunate marriage have made you *distraite, pauvrette.* And no wonder you feel the *mésalliance.* Fancy one's cousin marrying a governess !'

Maryanne's paternal grandfather, by the way, was commonly believed to have begun life as a costermonger.

'I wonder people can be bothered to marry in mid-summer,' murmured Moncrieff, in accents the most die-away. 'It is either raining or sweltering, and yet there is such a tediously long list every morning in the *Reflector.*'

'*Que voulez vous ?*' cried Maryanne.

'Nobody would marry in May, you know; everybody waits. Is my cousin Maggie Macklurkin's in to-day's *Reflector?*'

Moncrieff could not tell. Was she to be expected to charge her mind with other people's cousins' marriages?

'It wasn't in the *Newsman*,' said Maryanne. 'There isn't a *Reflector* in the house, I suppose; but might I send a servant for one? I should just like to see if Maggie's has been inserted.'

She might send a servant for one, if she would—Moncrieff cared not. So the servant was dispatched, and the *Reflector* brought, and, to the much gratification of Maryanne, 'Maggie's' did prove to have been inserted. Another marriage was there too, which had not been in the *Newsman;* the marriage at Hilyascord, Shetland, of Glen Cassillis of Baronshaugh to Christian, third daughter of the late Eric Elvester, Master of Eastravoe.

Moncrieff seemed to have nothing for her cousin's marriage but pettish silence.

Maryanne, however, had plenty to say about
the marriage of hers. Gossip averred that
there existed a family feud between the
respective households of Maryanne and
Maggie, and that the Macklurkins would
have no dealings with the Kirkpatricks; so
it must have been from hearsay that she
told this Netherlaw young lady how many
guineas her cousin's wedding-breakfast cost;
how much the presents were valued at;
the estimated price of the trousseau.

'Where is the sense of a trousseau?' lan-
guidly drawled Moncrieff, closing her eyes.

Her own paraphernalia would intensely
interest when its time should come; but
what to her was that of Maryanne's cousin
Maggie?

'*Ciel!*' ejaculated Miss Kirkpatrick, forgetting that she was not now in Paris; forgetting likewise that she was the daughter
of a douce elder of the United Presbyterian
persuasion, 'hasn't every bride a trousseau?
Hadn't even Miss Elvester something like
one?'

'I don't know; I've not seen her since she ran away from Argyll Gardens. She has been at Hilyascord nearly ever since she was engaged—Lady Trayll is her god-mother or something. Glen behaved very badly about a letter of mine—but I wrote you after the mistake, didn't I?'

'Yes, dear; but only once. You never told me how it ended.'

'It ended in Glen's marrying Miss Elves-ter, of course,' said Moncrieff.

'But what did your cousin Glen say to you, dear Moncrieff?' questioned Maryanne, coaxingly.

She was curious to hear all the outs and ins of that coil.

'He never spoke about the letter. Wasn't it spiteful? For then I could have explained, and everything' (Moncrieff showed signs of returning animation now), 'and if I ever named Miss Elvester to him, he became quite fierce—like some frightful, painted savage with a war-whoop.'

'It was all Miss Elvester's doing, you

may depend,' cried Maryanne, with much outward sympathy. 'I always told you she was sly, sly; and now you have truly found it. Captain Cassillis has been fairly caught, and nothing else—that is just what it is. Your poor Aunt Marjorie, how I pity her.'

'You needn't, for she is quite pleased. She has always wanted it.'

'Your Aunt Euphemia didn't want it, anyhow. Is she very angry with Miss Elvester and Captain Cassillis?'

'She is always very angry with everybody. But cousin Glen doesn't mind her, not in the least. You needn't call him Captain Cassillis, Maryanne; *I* never will, now that he has left the army, for I think it was rather grasping of him to take the property, when he knew that I was engaged to poor dear Quentin, who would have done anything for me.'

'But the entail, *très chère?*'

'Oh, I know; but entail is so stupid altogether. I don't see why one shouldn't have an estate as well as another. And I wish Parliament would pass an Act that people must not leave everything to their sons and nothing to their daughters, so that Dugald is quite nonsensically rich, while I have hardly enough to dress myself decently with.'

If this young person had possessed a wishing-cap, some startling phenomena would have resulted.

' How very disgusted your brother must be with your cousin's marriage,' observed Maryanne. ' What does he say about it ? '

She took a deep and undying interest in her friend's brother. No length of Dugald ever surfeited Miss Kirkpatrick.

One of Moncrieff's gifts was her knack of evading questions even the most direct, if to answer them would be at all troublesome to her. So she looked blankly in Maryanne's face, just as if she had never heard the inquiry, and said,—

' Dugald is going to stay in Shetland all this month.'

'The naughty wretch,' cried playful Maryanne. 'You should have been there, dear,
to keep him in order.'

'I was invited, of course, but I couldn't
go,' pouted Moncrieff.

'*Mais pourquoi?*' said Maryanne, and
forgetting that she was in Netherlaw.

'Because I'm such a bad sailor. I should
have been quite odiously ill; and I have
such a horror of sea-sickness. It would
make me look shocking for days afterwards.'

'Just why I didn't go to Maggie's,' rejoined Maryanne confidentially. 'I knew
I should look ill after newly having crossed
the Channel.' (She had never been invited
to Maggie's, if the truth were known.)

Moncrieff's notion was, that crossing the
Channel would not materially affect the appearance of one who never did or could,
under any circumstances, look well; and
that therefore Maryanne might have gone
to 'Maggie's' with an easy mind. But
that was a matter of no concern to her;
and ill-looks having suggested the subject,

she went on to a consideration of the misfortunes of being obliged to wear mourning; mingling her plaint with reminiscences of 'poor dear Quentin'—what a good creature he had been, and how devoted to her, and reflections against Netherlaw warehousemen for not having on hand the exact shades in lavender silk, which one imperatively required.

A loud peal resounding through the silent corridors, brought the interesting disquisition to an abrupt finish.

'That must be Glen,' said Moncrieff; 'but I'm sure he needn't make so much noise.'

'How—why—you told me he was perfectly certain not to arrive till after we had got away,' ejaculated Maryanne, hastily rising.

'Well, I wish he hadn't,' rejoined Moncrieff fretfully. 'But how could I know? Boats are ridiculously uncertain.'

'If I could only leave without being seen,' said Maryanne, in perplexity. 'Captain Cassillis will think it so very strange to meet me here.'

'I daresay he will,' agreed Moncrieff indifferently ; 'but never mind.'

It was vastly easy to say 'never mind,'
but Maryanne did mind a good deal. She
had no more than a bowing acquaintance
with the lady of the house, and it *would*
be awkward to be caught by that lady's
son taking tea in the back parlour. Unfortunately there was no escape for her.
To leave the room would only be to en-
counter Captain Cassillis in the hall. How
excessively annoying ! And the scrape had
not been fallen into through her own fault
either, but entirely through the misrepre-
sentations of that most idiotic Moncrieff.
Yet, indeed, when she came to consider it,
why need she be so greatly put out of
countenance ? Might she not fairly regard
herself as being above criticism ? in short,
was she not a Kirkpatrick ?

So she sat down again, dressed her face
with smiles, and blandly awaited the incoming
of the bride and bridegroom !

CHAPTER XIV.

DISUNITED.

'To marry one whom you could adore, and whose heart
is closed to you—to yearn for the treasure, and
only to claim the casket—to worship the statue that
you may never warm to life. Oh ! such a marriage
would be a hell, the more terrible because Paradise
was in sight.'

THE new Laird of Baronshaugh was
bringing his bride from Shetland,
where, owing to the extreme
urgency of the Traylls of Hilyascord, old
and valued family friends, the marriage
had been celebrated ; and celebrated with
as much state as if Christian had been still
an Elvester of Eastravoe.

Moncrieff had assured Maryanne that
the travellers would not reach Netherlaw

till late to-night. Why she thought this,
or whether she did think it, was known
only to herself. The real state of the case
was, that Glen and his wife ought to have
reached Netherlaw on the previous evening ; but a mist had delayed the Shetland
steamer fully twelve hours. So it had been
a tedious journey, and now to refresh themselves after it, they had Moncrieff.

The unexpectedness of the pleasure must
have somewhat influenced Glen's manner to
his cousin, for the young lady pettishly com-
plained. You don't look one bit pleased to
see me, cousin Glen.'

'Oh, I'm tremendously pleased,' he replied. 'My pleasure, however, is a matter
of secondary importance.'

And he stood aside to let Christian mani-
fest herself.

To Christian, therefore, Moncrieff was
obliged to turn her attention. She did not,
of course, agree about Glen's wife's pleasure
being of more importance than Glen's. That
was infinitely absurd. She gave Christian the

right hand of fellowship, however ; told her
that she looked 'quite dreadfully washed-
out'; asked her if she would have any
tea, and forget all about it the same minute.

But who now so exquisitely agreeable as
Miss Kirkpatrick, or so friendly to the bride!
In a style the most frankly delightful, she
accounted for her presence on the scene,
and from that proceeded to sympathise
with Christian for having had to undertake
a journey so fatiguing.

' Though, when one remembers the circumstances,' she added, with graceful wag-
gishness, ' it would not be fatiguing at all.'

Then she read aloud from the *Reflector*
the notification of the marriage at Hilyascord,
and remarked that it did ' sound so pretty.'

' When Aunt Euphemia saw it this
morning,' observed Moncrieff, ' she said you
must have telegraphed from Orkney ; and
she thought it was a judgment.'

' About the telegraphing, my aunt displayed her usual sagacity,' said Glen. ' But
the judgment clause is not clear to me.'

'She thought it so extravagant to telegraph,' explained his cousin. 'She says
you are turning out quite a shocking squan-
derer, and that it is a judgment on Aunt
Marjorie for not having brought you up
more strictly.'

If Moncrieff ever did chance to bear
in mind aught concerning a fellow-creature,
it was sure to be something of a disparaging
nature ; generally an offensive remark made
by somebody. But Mrs Sledgehammer's
animadversions did not trouble Glen.

'Well, Moncrieff, what about the tea you
spoke of?' he asked.

'Oh, I forgot,' said she ; 'but do you want
tea, cousin Glen ?'

'*I* don't, but I rather think somebody else
does. And while she's having it, I'll go
down to the club for letters.'

So Christian had the tea, and Glen went
to the club, and Maryanne, breathing a
benediction in French, departed, leaving
behind her an impression not quite so
favourable as she perhaps imagined ; her

change from superciliousness to suavity had not heightened Christian's at no time high opinion of her.

In Moncrieff there was no such change; and so soon as she and her cousin's wife were left alone together, the latter had to hear how very tiresome Maryanne was, always telling such stupid stories about such stupid things; and how unbusiness-like those Netherlaw shopkeepers were, never having in stock the shades one wanted; then the talk drifted into home grievances.

'Aunt Euphemia is staying at Craigie Urquhart this month,' Moncrieff said; 'it saves her the expense of a coast house. But she is so dreadfully, dreadfully tiresome, and Dr Sledgehammer is worse than a funeral. I wish Glen would ask them to Baronshaugh. Only, Aunt Euphemia might not go; for she says cousin Glen has furnished so extravagantly, that it makes her feel like the Prophet Jeremiah, or some other old person of that nation. And she says there will be a constant carnival or

saturnalia or some such thing, where she
and Quentin used to live so quietly.   Poor,
dear cousin Quentin !'

' I daresay Glen and I shall live rather
quietly too,' said Christian.

' If you do, visiting at Baronshaugh will
be very dull and stupid,' argued Moncrieff.
' It used to be quite fearful in poor, dear
Quentin's life.   If it hadn't been so slow,
you would never have been married to
cousin Glen ; for if anybody had done anything to entertain me, I should not have
written the letter.'

Christian did not apprehend the allusion.

' Don't you know about *that ?*' said Moncrieff, discontentedly ; to explain was always
a very great hardship to her.   ' And yet
Glen has been so nasty to me about it ; he
must have told you, Miss Elvester.'

' Indeed not,' replied Christian ; ' but
never mind, it can't matter at all that I
should know.'

' Haven't you seen for yourself that Glen
was an admirer of mine ?' questioned Mon-

crieff, in a somewhat querulous fashion. 'And don't you know that he hoped to marry me in time?'

'No, I don't.'

'You can ask him if he didn't, then,—and you'll see.'

Christian smiled.

'Oh, he would never have *thought* of *you*, if he hadn't got that letter,' pursued Moncrieff.

'I ought to be obliged to the writer of that letter,' said Christian. 'Is it to you I must make my acknowledgments?'

'It was a letter I had written to Mary-anne Kirkpatrick, telling her that I was engaged to cousin Quentin,' rejoined Moncrieff. 'Glen got it by mistake and read it. (*So* mean of him!) Till then he had always hoped I would marry him, but when he saw I was going to marry cousin Quentin instead (I daresay we mightn't have been married after all—Quentin was ever a waverer), he made himself quite diabolically disagreeable, and went at once and proposed to you. That was his spiteful way.'

This account of the letter and Glen's spite
had merely come in by-the-bye; there was
no preconcerted plan about it. Moreover,
Moncrieff no doubt believed in the statement she had made; that every young man
who looked at her should wish to marry her
was of course. And at Quentin's death she
would certainly have become engaged to the
next laird, had it not been for that most
unlucky letter. Yet she was not vindictive;
there was not even any passion in her utterance; her tone rather resembled that of
an aggrieved child, who fretfully remembers that some time since it possessed a toy
which it has now lost.

The words fell as an idle tale on Christian's ears; for Moncrieff, everybody knew,
imagined so much. The thought did cross
her mind, 'What if this were true!' But it
passed like a flash. Glen could not be
guilty of such deceitfulness; Glen was above
suspicion.

'Cousin Glen *is* so very odd, you know,'
continued Moncrieff, after drawing breath;

'but he is a great match for you, isn't he, Miss Elvester?'

'Do you think so?' said Christian. 'At any rate, I had engaged myself to him before I knew he would be what you call a great match for me and I should have been better; pleased to marry him so, than I have been to marry him as he is, because then everybody must have known that it was only for himself.'

This pretty bride-like enthusiasm was to Moncrieff so many meaningless words; and she put it aside as only some more of the ridiculousness which she found so much of in the earth, and passed to another subject, asking what Christian would recommend her to wear at a grand entertainment to be given by the Baillie Geddes family at their newly-erected castle in the hill country. She had put the same question to every fresh person whom she had met for the last three weeks, would go on doing so for the three weeks next to come, and the matter would finally be settled for her by her maid.

'Some people wonder at me for going there,' she said, after Christian, knowing all the while how useless it was, had given an opinion on the toilet difficulty. 'And Dugald is quite speechless. He says he can't stand those vulgar rich, and that, undesirable as the Kirkpatricks are, the Baillie Geddes set is a great deal worse. But then Dugald is such a poky person, don't you think? Anyhow, the eldest Baillie Geddes girl is engaged to Sir Leveret Landless of Hungerscarth. His property is all mortgaged, you know, and he only has an allowance; but Baillie Geddes is going to make him all right, if he marries his daughter. He is quite an Adonis, Maryanne Kirkpatrick says, but a gambler. Would you marry a gambler, Miss Elvester? I never would, unless I could be sure he would always win. I have had eleven offers in all—no, twelve; but let me count.'

And she began to reckon up the list on her fingers. While she was thus employed, her cab came; so she had to relinquish the

pleasing task in the middle—for trains, like
time and tide, wait for no man—and leave
the exact number of her offers an open
question, with a leaning to the side of twelve.
At the hall door she met Glen, and for
the first time remembered to inquire for
her Aunt Marjorie.

'I refer you to Miss Elvester,' replied
Glen; 'she has seen far more of my mother
lately than I have.'

Christian had not minded being called
by her old name so long as it was only
Moncrieff who called her by it; but 'Miss
Elvester' from Glen was a different matter;
it was just such a mistake as he might
make, if he *had* married her under the influence of pique at another woman's deser-
tion. But he never noticed his own slip;
an omission on the part of Moncrieff called
for his attention.

'Haven't you forgotten something?' he
said, as his cousin was about to pass through
the doorway.

'What have I forgotten?' she cried.

'Martha has charge of all my parcels. How teasing you are ! *What* have I forgotten, Glen ? '

'Only to say good-evening to—' and he led her back into the hall and turned her about to face Christian, who stood by one of the pillars, looking on.

'It wasn't worth bringing you back for, was it?' said the bride.

Moncrieff evidently considered that it was not. She held out her hand, however, and seemed to mean to kiss Christian (who ignored that intention), and wished a second time that the Sledgehammers would relieve Craigie Urquhart of their dismal presence, and gingerly took her way down the wet steps. Then, with characteristic indifference to everybody but herself, she was completely surprised to find that her cousin did not propose to accompany her further than across the pavement. She would have taken her departure without missing him if he had not been on the spot; but having so timeously returned, what was he for but to pleasure her.

' You are coming to Royal Street, surely ? ' she said, making room for him by her side.

The coolness of her could not but provoke a smile.

' It's not necessary,' said Glen ; ' you have your maid.'

' I haven't—at least she's above. Besides, a maid is nothing.'

' Just try for once to imagine that she is something ; by striving very hard, who knows but you may succeed ? '

Moncrieff drew her eyebrows together.

' You used to be so very much more agreeable,' she said.

' I'm sorry to have deteriorated ; but even yet I am not so bad as I might be, for I don't want you to miss your train, which you certainly will if I detain you longer. Commend me to the Sledgehammers. And be a good girl, Moncrieff. Good-bye.'

While Moncrieff, in a very bad temper with her provoking cousin, was driving through the rain to Royal Street, Glen joined Christian at the back window, whither

she had gone to contemplate the drizzle.
He put the tips of his fingers under her
chin, and so raised her face that he could
study it at convenience.　Then he shook
his head.

'You ought to have been resting,' he said,
'for the journey has fatigued you.　You are
paler than I like to see.'

'You know what happens to eyes that
look at the sun,' she answered brightly; 'it
is not so much that I have lost colour, as
that you have been looking at the sun.'

'Is that all?　I wish I could be sure of
it.　Had Moncrieff offended you seriously,
Christian, that you dismissed her as you
did?'

'Offended me?　No.　And what do you
mean by "dismissed her as you did?"　I
did not dismiss her—she went.'

'You were so provokingly cool to her, I
mean, my little lady; you drew yourself up
with such an air when she would have
kissed you.　I never saw anything quite so
grand before.'

' I did not mean it, Glen; I would not knowingly put on airs. And I did not kiss your cousin, only because I never do kiss any but those whom I am really fond of.'

' Never? And if one whom you are not fond of should by some perversity of fate be fond of you, and so desire to kiss; how then ?'

' I must let her, I suppose. But one who, like your cousin, rather dislikes me than not, shall not—no, not even if by some perversity of fate I care a very great deal for her.'

' Which you do not for my cousin. Does she weary you very much, Christian ?'

' I weary her more than she wearies me; she amuses me sometimes.'

' How did she amuse you to-day ?'

The question was asked in an off-hand fashion enough, but Christian, very quick to interpret Glen, perceived that he still retained the impression that, with or without reason, his wife was angry with his cousin. To remove this mistaken idea, nothing, it seemed to her, would serve so well as to repeat to him, in jest, as much as he would have of Moncrieff's conversation. So she said, lightly,—

'Your cousin amused me to-day by telling me what I should never otherwise have found out. *Now* I've been informed why you married me : a letter fell into your hands by mischance ; I needn't say what it was about, only that it made you come to me with—O! Glen, Glen—'

The recital gaily begun, ended in a startled cry, as Christian, feeling the hand in which both of hers were enclosed suddenly tighten, looked up and saw that her husband's face had grown crimson, and that there was an expression that could mean only one thing in his eyes.

'Well, my dearest?' he asked, with as much carelessness as he could assume.

'Tell me that it is not true,' she said entreatingly, but at the same time drawing her hands away from him. 'You could not, *you*—have deceived me so.'

Instead of answering this, he mentally

anathematised Moncrieff for the pretty piece of mischief she had made. Reasoning from general observation of his cousin, he had believed that more recent events must by this time have crowded out the circumstances of All-Fool's Day from among the things that were of interest strong enough to be spoken about by her. But it is never safe to calculate upon what will or will not be done in any unusual situation by such a one as Moncrieff. Having got no reply, Christian covered her face and ejaculated in faint, broken accents of distress,—

'If I had known sooner—but now—now —what shall I do?'

Then Glen tried to draw the trembling hands from before the downcast face, but could not; then he would have put his arms about her, but she shuddered and almost passionately besought him to let her alone.

'I really do not understand you,' he said.

And the remark was truer than he knew.

'Was it indeed because you read the letter

that you asked me to be your wife?' she inquired.

'It was because I fully believed what I do yet fully believe, that I was acting for the best, that I asked you to be my wife.'

'I don't know what you call "the best,"' she said. 'Can it be best for me to be married to a man who did not want me? or for you to have married a woman whom you do not care for, while you—'

'Love another,' she would have added, but the words choked her and would not pass her lips.

'But I do care for you,' he responded. 'I swear it, Christian; and but for this random talk of Moncrieff's, you should never have had the shadow of a reason for doubting my regard.'

He did 'care' for her; but for Moncrieff's random talk, she should never have had the shadow of a reason for doubting his 'regard.' But this did not comfort Christian. What matter that Glen did after an easy fashion care for her? She would rather have nothing at all from him than such ' regard.'

Her dream of happiness had, while it lasted, been very sweet. But what an awakening! Her king of men had discrowned himself. Glen had mocked her by the gift of his name, while his love had long before been given to Moncrieff. Shaken as her faith was, however, she still held to the belief that the man would never forget that a wife stood between him and his cousin now. But this did not for the present make much difference to her. Nothing could as yet alleviate the pain of knowing that Glen had lightly held out his hand to her—*to her!*—only in order that he might be revenged on the butterfly who had thrown him over; and the bitterness of it was, if possible, made the more bitter by finding that she, proud as she was too, was quite expected by her husband to be meekly contented with his ' regard.' So a sense of humiliation mingled with the misery of disappointed love. Poor Christian! the sun had gone down for her at noonday, and she was left shivering in the dark.

She neither wept nor declaimed ; she sat tearless and still, with a settled despair on her face, wondering why Glen should go on trying to make his peace with her, and how he could be so little ashamed of what he had done. At first he had been sufficiently disconcerted no doubt—it was his own face only which had betrayed him,—but he had recovered himself almost immediately, and now, to hear him talk, one would think that he did not at all comprehend the reason of such sharp distress.

And neither, in truth, he did. Glen was under a complete misapprehension. He never supposed (how could he ?) that Moncrieff had spoken of him as a lover of hers. What he imagined was, that his cousin had kept to the real fact, as thus,—' Your husband must have married you because, in the letter spoken of, he saw it stated that you loved him, and stated so that he did not doubt its truth.' And to a proud, sensitive

girl such a discovery must have come with a
shock. Vexation was natural; vexation,
however, which would gradually give way
under the influence of soothing words, and
endearments, and protestations of 'regard.'
But this deep-seated resentment was more
than the circumstances called for. Christian blamed him for having deceived her.
She had so entirely believed in him, and
all the while he had only been deceiving
her, she pathetically said. Yet he could not
vindicate himself by answering,—'The deception you complain of was resorted to in
order to secure your happiness. Unless I
had held back part of the truth from you,
you would not have agreed to marry me.
You yourself ought to see this, and so to
desist from your unreasonable anger.' Instead of plain-speaking like this, Glen had
to deal in ambiguities and generalities; and
these Christian paid no attention to, thinking
them so utterly inconsequent. Her mind
was full of one idea, his of another; therefore, as was only natural, they quite missed

each other.   He considered her unjust; she
looked upon him as unpardonable.

The bride's state of mind may be gathered
from the fact that she was actually unwilling
to go on to Baronshaugh.   Her marriage
had been a mockery; she did not see how
she could act it out, she said.

Glen looked at her incredulously when it
came to that.

'Do you intend me to go to Baronshaugh
without you? to Baronshaugh or anywhere
else?' he asked.   'Because, if that *is* your
meaning, let me assure you that I will do
nothing so mad.   You may suppose it necessary to proclaim to the world that you have
quarrelled with me, but I don't happen to
share your opinion as to the expediency of
that.'

'It is not a quarrel, this,' she said.   'It is
only that I have been cruelly deceived by
you.   Can I help feeling it, do you think?'

He had already exhausted his eloquence,
trying to bring her to terms, and here she
was, woman-like, going back to the very

starting-point, and, with the licence of speech claimed by her sex, accusing him of cruelty added to deception. He was tired of it; he had not conceived her capable of such childishness; even sympathy failed him now.

'Whatever your purpose may be,' he said, 'mine is to perform the vows which I took upon me the other day. You are my wife, and I will never give you up. (To think that you could dream of proposing it!) Please let me hear no more of anything so impossible.'

Yes, she was his wife, there was no altering that; and even if he had deceived her, most cruelly, her place was henceforth by his side. She had spoken unadvisedly, but the voice of calm reason must now be listened to; and, listening, Christian admitted herself to be wrong, and acknowledged the necessity of keeping the breach between her and Glen a secret from the world.

CHAPTER XV.

BRIDEGROOMLESS.

'Return, return, O mournful, mournful bride;
Return and dry thy useless sorrow.'

BOUT eight o'clock that evening, Christian sat in a railway carriage at the River Street Station. She was alone, Glen having gone to see about securing the whole compartment. He had been away some time, and seemed in no haste to return. The guard, in his course of door-slamming, came, but had to pass on without the ceremony of seeing the ticket; then the bell rang, and Christian said to herself,—'I daresay he will be too late.'

She almost wished he would; for, when
evil has fallen upon you, you sometimes have
a reckless feeling that matters had better just
be a little worse when they are about it.
What is the use of anything at all going
right when so much else has gone wrong?
She kept her place, therefore, and watched
from her window the humours of the busy
platform, wondering the while if, among all
those men and women walking up and down,
there was one other such a heavy heart as
hers. A bride and bridegroom stood full in
view; an obtrusively enamoured pair, so
new-fangled that they could not keep their
honeymoon happiness to themselves, but
were taking all the travelling public into
their confidence. The sight was too much
for this other and less fortunate bride, and
her eyes filled. But such weakness would
never do, must be put a stop to at once; so
Christian brushed away the tears before they
fell. As she did this, a black-coated figure
emerged from the crowd, invaded Christian's
compartment, and next moment Mrs Cassil-

lis of Baronshaugh found herself contraven-
ing the company's bye-laws by travelling
without a ticket.

Glen had indeed missed the train ; careless
Glen ! and there would be none other to-
night.   But it did not matter ; nothing
mattered now ; let the very worst betide, and
Christian would bear it with stoicism.   The
worst ?   Glen absent, not through carelessness, but because ' something had happened '
to him ; could she stoically endure such a
worst as that ?   Scarcely, it is to be doubted ;
for at the mere idea of the contingency, her
heart went fast and faster.

The other occupant of the carriage was
none else than Mrs Brackenburn's pet aver-
sion, the Rev. Daniel Carnegy, of Braidmoss.
This gentleman made a conscience of drawing a bow at a venture, wherever he might
be ; so, after covertly observing his fellow-
passenger for some time and marking the
intensity of the gaze which she directed
towards the iron-works amidst which the
route lay, he politely put into her hands a

weekly religious periodical, entitled 'Zion's Trump,' with the remark, that it might be she would find matter of interest therein.

Christian knew the minister of Braidmoss by sight, and was aware that he had a habit of offering ghostly council and instruction to whoever would lend him an ear; but she was not exactly prepared to talk over her most private feelings with any man. She gladly accepted the periodical as an equivalent for conversation, therefore, and abstractedly turned the leaves. For frontispiece there was the by no means alluring portrait of Bounding Bill, the Converted Acrobat. Then came a record of the great work being done by that evangelist among the masses of Netherlaw. Besides this there were many surprising, not to say sensational, scenes and incidents, most graphically described. The question : Is it seemly in a clergyman to wear a ring ? was discussed, and settled in the negative; the date of the battle of Armageddon was definitely fixed; and full details

given of the Millennium. In short, 'Zion's
Trump' stood in the same place to one portion of the community as the Penny Dreadful to another.

Christian followed the words with her
eyes ; but her mind was far from them. Her
anxiety was great. Her king had discrowned himself ; but still, but still—

At Braidmoss a telegram relieved her.
Glen regretted that he had lost the train ;
would follow early to-morrow ; had telegraphed to the people at the hotel to have
a carriage in waiting to convey Christian
to Baronshaugh.

So the bride went to her new home alone ;
and Laighbield gossiped ; and on the following Sunday Mr Carnegy, who turned every
trivial incident to pulpit use, and sucked a
moral from each, as Jacques sucked melan-
choly from a song, told his congregation
about the ticketless traveller from Netherlaw,
and drew a parallel between the Braidmoss
railroad and the railroad of life, wherein he
showed that the grand difference between

these lay in the fact that, while on the former
the want of a ticket could easily be made up
for, on the latter it would fare ill with those
who were found without a passport at the
terminus.

CHAPTER XVI.

FRIENDS.

'They made a paction 'tween them twa,
   They made it firm and sure, O.'

NEXT morning betimes Glen came riding through the grounds of the goodly inheritance which had fallen to him. On emerging from the maze of trees by which the house was hidden, and getting into the clear space in front, he glanced up and down the many windows, as if thinking that at one of them he might see his bride watching for him. If he did expect this, he was disappointed; for no bride was there. But on his way back from the stables, he looked casually along a right wing of the mansion, without any expectation this time, and did catch a glimpse of Christian at an open casement.

She leant forward, with her hands outside among the roses which climbed the wall, so that her wedding-ring shone in the sunlight like a circlet of golden flame. It was a charming picture, the fair girl's head and bust in frame of bloom and greenery. The face was one which it would be well worth a man's while to see flushing and growing eager at his approach. Perhaps it had done so before to-day for Glen; but not now. Now, if it flushed at all, it was not from tenderness, and if it disappeared quickly from amongst the foliage, it was not that Christian might hasten to bid her husband welcome. Not thus, indeed. If it so pleased him, he might come to her; she need not, and would not go to him.

During the past twelve hours she had fully considered her position. Her attitude towards the husband who had deceived her was decided upon. Now to practise it.

Not knowing what sort of reception might

be awaiting him, Glen proceeded to the
morning-room. It was full of sunshine—
the early shining which brightens, but does
not burn—and of the scent of flowers from
the garden beneath. General gladness prevailed ; the hum of bees came up cheerily ;
butterflies intoxicated with pleasure fluttered
by ; birds from every branch twittered satisfaction with this brightness after rain. And,
as far as could be seen, there was nothing
about Christian out of harmony with nature's
rejoicing. She had put sighs and tears
behind her, and wore a face as fresh as the
roses which peeped in at her window. Seated
in a low wicker chair by the open casement,
she heard her husband come along the cor-
ridor ; and, when the door opened, she slowly
rose. It had been her desire to get through
her part without any semblance of constraint ;
but that she could not quite ; and, instead of
going forward as she had meant, stood still,
contemplating the tip of her tiny slipper
and playing rather nervously with the cord
and tassels of her apron. Whatever Glen's

misgivings might be, there was certainly no
nervousness in his manner. He shook hands
just as he used to do when Christian was
still Miss Elvester, and just as he would have
explained a matter to her then, he said,—

'Now; hear my defence. It was *not* my
fault that you had to leave Netherlaw alone
last night.'

'No matter about it,' she replied. 'You
see it has not harmed me in the least.'

This was no pretence, either; there did
not lurk the faintest suspicion of anything
disagreeable in those pleasant low tones.

'But I'm sorry we were separated, all the
same,' said Glen. 'This is how it was: a
child was run over by a hansom at the
entrance of the station, and I had to pick
him up. It had got to be done, you see;
and I, as the man nearest, was bound to
do it.'

'Of course you were,' rejoined Christian,
looking straight up into his eyes, her own
full of interest. 'And the unfortunate little
child,—what of him ?'

'He was taken to the infirmary, and will do very well. A special Providence watches over street waifs.'

Christian was not satisfied with this generalisation. She must hear the whole circumstances; for she had often looked at and thought about those Netherlaw street waifs. Glen gave the required details to her, and having done so, remarked,—

'So you see I could not help myself. But alone as you were, you got here without trouble, I suppose?'

'Yes, thanks; you had arranged to save me that.'

'I hoped so. And I had a telegram from the hotel when you left Braidmoss; otherwise I shouldn't have been able to feel quite comfortable about you last night.'

She readily guessed why. But there were certain subjects best avoided; so she remarked upon the loveliness of the morning, and expressed her pleasure that the rain and the clouds were gone. A silence succeeded, during which Christian resumed her wicker-

chair at the window ;—for, in circumstances
which threaten to become embarrassing, a
window, when the situation permits, is one's
natural refuge ; a child, a dog, a cat, may
serve, but should none of these be in the
way, then certainly the window.

Glen did not know what to make of the
change of mood, but could only surmise that
his bride had come to see the unreason-
ableness of her anger. It was well ; though
with satisfaction surprise somewhat mingled ;
surprise that that should be entirely con-
doned to-day, which but yesterday had
been declared unpardonable ; still, it was
well.

Looking at his wife now, and assuming
from the expression of her face that he
might proceed to claim a husband's due, he
went across, and saying,—

'Allow me, sweet,' stooped to serve himself to a kiss. 'He was quickly shown his
mistake. Christian grew as red as a rose, and
she visibly trembled ; but would *she* permit
such an attention from one who offered it

VOL. II.

merely because he had an idea that it was in the bond?

'You must not!—you shall not!' she said, with quickened breath and head thrown back.

'But why?' he demanded, laying hold of her, as she rose to get away from him.

'I beg you to let me go,' she only said.

'First, tell me why I should. What are you afraid of? Am I really not to have the kiss, Christian?'

His grasp was tighter than he was aware, and he did not think of the rings on the hands he held, nor know that he was inflicting pain, till Christian exclaimed,—

'You hurt me, Captain Cassillis!'

'A million pardons!' he cried, and let go straightway. 'Have I done much mischief?'

'It is nothing,' she replied, 'only it was painful at the moment;' and after just glancing at the finger upon which a diamond star had left its impression, she hid her hand in the pocket of her apron.

'I am sincerely sorry,' said Glen. 'I

would not wittingly cause you a moment's pain, even though you are so undutiful.'

Her lip curled ever so slightly, and she thought,—

'Undutiful, indeed! Undutiful!'

'And this is your idea of how to treat a husband,' observed Glen, leaning against the wall with folded arms, and regarding his bride with a kind of amused curiosity; for he was scarcely inclined to take the matter seriously.

Christian answered nothing, only withdrew beyond arm's-length and looked back over her shoulder, as if daring him to follow her. Interpreting the look so, Glen said,—

'Excuse me, but this goes a short way past a jest.'

'It is no jest, indeed,' she rejoined. 'I am very much in earnest.'

'You are!'

Christian turned and faced him then.

'I am,' she said.

'Well, I too can be very much in earnest; and I feel half inclined to have that kiss in spite of you. I could easily take it, Christian.'

'Oh, but you will not,' she responded, still holding him at bay with a pair of such clear, grave eyes. 'I am not afraid; you are too manly to put your strength to such a use.'

'Why is this?' he asked. 'Do you quite hate me?'

She knew that he did not, could not, think she hated him; and she also knew, or believed she knew, which came practically to the same thing, that he did not really desire a kiss from her, but made this little ado only because an unexpected difficulty had been thrown in the way of obtaining one.

'I don't hate you at all,' she answered, lowering her eyelids, while once more a deeper colour swept her face. 'It does not follow that one hates a man, because one will not have him kiss her.'

Glen was silent for an instant, rather disposed to be angry, then the comic aspect of the case struck him, and he laughed.

'This is very hard on me,' he said. 'Was ever any fellow served so unkindly? But I have been allowed to kiss you before now; have you forgotten it, Christian?'

'Have *you* forgotten yesterday?' asked Christian, speaking very low, and shading her too tell-tale face with a gay Japanese hand-screen which had lain conveniently by.

'There is no cause why yesterday should not be forgotten,' he replied, 'but the very best why it should.'

'Ah, if it could be!' she rejoined. 'But think, Glen; when a girl discovers that she is the wife of a man who has—' she paused to pick her words, for she did not want to weaken her self-justification by the use of too strong language.

'Well?' he said ironically. 'Who has an interesting habit of making short work with the Decalogue every now and then, I suppose you mean.'

'No; I only mean, who has concealed from her what, if known, would have made it impossible for her to marry him, she is not

likely to forget; and she can't be expected
to be so dutiful—since you call it being dutiful—as other wives are.'

When Glen had once already told Christian
that he did care for her, she had treated the
information in a style which showed that it
was not lukewarm caring for she wanted;
that it was all or nothing she would have.
He therefore made no second mention of the
caring, but he said,—

'Have I not assured you that you shall
have no cause to complain of me? But let
me repeat it: I will do all that man may to
make you happy; only give me leave to
try.'

'Thank you,' she replied, half-smiling;
'but I shall not trouble you so far. I quite
mean to be as happy as I can; but you must
kindly let me find happiness by myself, and
in my own way.'

'By yourself? That implies that you won't
have anything to say to me at all? My dear
Mrs Cassillis, you seem to be a person of
most advanced ideas. Will you bow to me

when we meet by chance on the staircase or about the grounds ?'

'That as you like,' she answered, accommodatingly.

'Oh no ; but as you like,' said Glen.

'Well, then ; we have been tolerably good friends all along ; let us be so still.'

'Ah, yes ; a most charming and desirable arrangement,' observed Glen, raising his eyebrows.

'If it isn't charming and desirable, it is at least better than if you went on acting at being my lover any longer,' said Christian. 'And now, please, won't we talk of something else ? Tell me if I may have Willie Ruthven here to amuse me during these long summer days.'

'Need you ask ? If he is to form an element in your happiness, by all means have him without delay,' said Glen.

But for all that, he did not see the desirability of the thing himself. It was, in truth, a little annoying for him to find that the flower he had gathered—too carelessly, perhaps, but certainly with the best possible intentions—refused to be worn in his button-hole, but proudly elected to remain much farther apart from him than so. He had spoken of taking the kiss his wife would not grant; but he had not for one moment seriously entertained the thought. In such a case as this, if persuasion were powerless, force was as entirely out of the question. Christian must follow her caprice, then, unheard of as it was. She would tire of it by-and-by, without doubt. In the meantime, it might prove a somewhat amusing performance, on the whole—a kind of drawing-room comedetta for two; and Glen was vain enough to imagine that *his* part in it would not be the more difficult to play.

END OF VOL. II.

COLSTON AND SON, PRINTERS, EDINBURGH.

www.ingramcontent.com/pod-product-compliance
Lightning Source LLC
Chambersburg PA
CBHW030338270326
41926CB00009B/882